DISCIPLINES OF THE

HOLY QUEST

FROM THE WISE AND THE STRONG

EDITED BY

FLOWER A. NEWHOUSE

THE CHRISTWARD MINISTRY
20560 QUESTHAVEN RD.
ESCONDIDO, CALIFORNIA 92025

Printed in the United States of America

DISCIPLINES OF THE HOLY QUEST

THE IMMORTAL ASCENT   BY J. OTTO SCHWEIZER

CONTENTS

Illustrations on pages 2, 12, 136, 152 and 174

FOREWORD

*"God is my witness whom I serve with my
spirit in the gospel of His Son."—Romans* 1:9

As a child, I saw colors, forms and persons that
others did not see. I was six years old when I
made the discovery that my family and playmates
did not possess extrasensory perception. This discovery stunned me and I ceased speaking to others
about lives and images which are normal to the
higher dimensions.

In my girlhood I felt a veritable command from
deep within to speak again of holy realities. Some
who heard did not understand. There were many,
however, who listened with eagerness and gladness, for the teachings which were given to me in
full conscious awareness had meaning and value
for these seekers. Most of this group of responsive
aspirants are still with us. To them, as to us, instructions from Souls who are wise and strong have
added meaning, beauty and purpose to life.

While receiving these instructions, I observed
the Teacher and received His thoughts as they
were spoken into my mind. Great Souls of this cal-
iber convey their wishes by telepathic thought

7

transference. The seed ideas are implanted in a prepared consciousness where they are translated into the language and vocabulary of the pupil.

How important it is that men realize that Masterhood did not begin and end in a single valiant soul! Mastership was attained by worthy candidates both before and after the birth of Christ. Our Lord is Lord of Angels and of men, and is Hierarch of the Christ Office; yet the purpose of evolution indicates that *every* individual is an apprentice of Masterhood. Moreover, Mastership has been attained by a slowly expanding group of perfected individuals. A few of these souls live useful, though necessarily unassuming lives on earth. Others serve specific Divine objectives in the higher dimensions. Always there are those who are concerned about mankind and its urgent need of redemption and improvement. Masters of this order watch for signs of human beings coming of age spiritually. They choose pupils who are found to contain uncompromising integrity in character and who have natures strongly endowed with reverence, responsiveness and humility. This character combination, plus a pioneering mind and spirit furnish a natural readiness for spiritual service.

Arthur Learned's artistic portrayals of the Wise and the Strong who are responsible for the lessons are included in the text. The drawings will reveal no names for the reason that knowing the names of Holy Ones gives a human being access to their attention. Few there are who are ready to be entrusted with specific name designations. Nevertheless, the pictures will help to introduce you to *very real persons* of remarkable spiritual stature whose instruction you may now study and safely practice. Each of these great servers is pledged to the Christ and to assisting Him in the ushering in of His vast and glorious kingdom on earth.

In the frontispiece, J. Otto Schweizer portrays two questers who have journeyed together Godward through innumerable centuries. They are pressing forward to their goal with unyielding determination. Their attitude of disinterest in regard to their tempters causes the evil forces to lose their vitality—to fade away as drooping figures bereft of influence. Nothing can delay or harm these fearless climbers whose one-pointed will to attain is the Light which clears every step as it is mounted.

The lessons which follow are self-explanatory. They describe some of the stimulating experiences and challenging requirements met by the earnest aspirant on his upward climb toward discipleship or holy obedience. Here are concise and explicit suggestions for living creatively close to God. A large manuscript houses the lessons from which these notes are taken. We believe there are hosts of individuals everywhere who seek the living Light from Souls who have outgrown earth's needs. For these many truth-hungry persons, knowledge of the way of discipleship will have genuine value.

This volume is designed as a manual for slow, careful study accompanied by the reader's sincere desire to apply the lessons in daily living. Accumulated knowledge *without assimilation* often leads to ineffectual congestion of the mind. These lessons are intended to help the earnest aspirant become a conscious, dedicated wielder of the Light in service to Christ, the Lord whose Way we follow.

We who use these instructions daily realize an ever-growing wonder, and an ever-expanding appreciation for truth shared with man from the summit of Mastership. Frequently we prepare for meditation by reviewing our treasured relationship to the Christ Hierarchy. You may find it helpful to preface each study period with preparatory thoughts similar to these:

"A great Hierarchy or Council of Perfected Souls exists. This group has jurisdiction over the lives constituting mankind. Even I am known to this body. Although I may not be fully aware of all its activities, still I know that It is and that I am responsible to It. In an affirmation of consecration and in thanksgiving, I open myself to a reception of beauties, powers and benefits from this constant center."

FLOWER A. NEWHOUSE

ONE OF THE WISE AND THE STRONG   BY ARTHUR G. LEARNED

THE CENTER OF INNER PEACE

Days are of little consequence unless you objectively come closer to the shining nearness of God's Presence Indwelling.

FIND your inner center—the center of your inward selves. When you have found that heart of your real individuality, you will know how to think, how to react, and how to bless those who constitute your present world. Let this be your effort: *Learn to keep centered.*

Do not let the pendulum of your endeavors sway too much to the right or left, but hold it poised within and cause its actions to be directed by your spiritual will. In other words, permit yourself only that freedom of action which can be controlled and maintained by your inward self. Let this be your effort this day; and if you will think of the Lord Christ, your Elder Brother in God, He will give you help.

A PORTENTOUS day to you! Concentrate this day on remembrance of the act of stilling yourself from the center within. In the western world, and especially in your century, you realize all too little

13

of the culture of serenity. This you are heartily en-
joined to exercise now. Realize through creative
contemplation such variations as meditations upon
stillness from the innermost to the outermost regions of consciousness, modes of conduct, modes of
action.

Devote ten minutes to reflection upon attaining
stillness for the next two hours as fully as possible—
mentally, emotionally and physically. Where it
is needful to be active physically, you can express
to the highest of your ability a greater degree of
calmness and of repose from the center of yourself.
Those who wear occidental bodies are restless, and
their radiations are distorted because of a lack of
aligned control from the center of their being.
Your physical body, recall, is not your center; neither are your feelings, nor your mentality. Your
center is above and beyond the mind, yet the mind
needs to open its gate in receptivity in order to allow the entrance of Light from that sphere which
is higher than mind—the Soul sphere.

During another period of remembrance you are
advised to reflect creatively upon such a theme as
quiet service done self-forgetfully during the next
two-hour period. Try to see yourself for two hours,
or four or six hours, being unself-conscious, repose-
ful, completely aware and in adoration of the all-
embracing Infinite Light of God.

In one of your remembrances you might experiment upon being self-contained and completely attuned to the Everlasting—wholly and positively aligned to the real, yet still appearing passive, impersonal, modest and free to an ever-expanding extent from the stimuli of the outer world.

Encourage intuitional impressions to flow into you from the Everlasting. Be responsive to them and conscious of their activity when they are impressing you.

During another time reflect upon the stillness in nature's beauty, such as a rose in bloom, a garden in the moonlight, deep lakes, or pine-crested peaks. Recall persons who, though extremely energetic and successful in their abilities to serve, are nevertheless tranquil or peace-imparting individuals. These are hints as to how you may learn to improve your poise and relaxation creatively.

On every occasion that you exercise purposeful remembrance, doors are opened into at-one-ment with a dynamic current of refreshment, and ability is increased with ever deepening sincerity.

REMEMBER, to unfold true discipleship requires alignment with your central self. You can, through one-pointed effort, slowly mount those states of consciousness that are necessary to reach the innermost Holy of Holies residing within. When you touch the fringes of the kingdom of your real self you will experience joy and relaxation such as you cannot find on any other level. *Continue to search for alignment with your true center where the real in you abides unceasingly.* You will know when you are centered because peace will be strong—a vital and pulsating peace which acts with strength in its own realm.

Another means by which you may touch the real within you is to dwell for a few minutes within the inclusiveness of your Soul Self. Lift up all your thoughts, feelings and energies into its domain of peace. Let the door open between your actual individuality and the other aspects or faculties of your whole being. You need courage, resolve and purposefulness to climb back to your centered self as often as possible.

Do not be afraid to express the best of yourself, to open and unfold all the tendrils of its blossoming to those around you. Then the bloom of the real shall grow in mighty strength and shall be conditioned with constant practice to stand the blasts of the chaotic world and the storms of unrest which lie in others.

LET your morning be new with objectivity.

Try to remember the Lord Christ and His Council of Masters at least every hour. Think of your Elder Brothers together as an assembly sending God Light in special beams into the sacred and meaningful places of earth. One of these beams shines through every retreat, chapel, church or cathedral sincerely dedicated to God. You need to remember today that wherever you are you may move in a beam which enfolds and penetrates you with its sustaining Light. Your purpose now is simply to remember this beam and your standing within it, and your being thoroughly aligned through it with the great assembly of Perfected, serving Souls.

Your hourly remembrance should consist of a desire to know the will and do that will of the Hierarchy. These requirements constitute a purpose the nature of which is to keep you inwardly aware of the transcendent spiritual love and helpfulness that surrounds you at all times.

LET us concern ourselves today with the unfoldment of creative receptivity to the inner worlds. This realization is developed by inner and outer stillness maintained while focusing attention upon God's threshold without allowing the mind to descend for any length of time to human levels and considerations. There are very few who can, without much effort, distinguish the salient forces projected from loftier planes of the eternal. Usually human beings are insensitive to these potent energies because they have not developed the interest sufficient to ground these vibrant thought impulses into the human aura. So these thought forms weave

17

in and out of the aura, moving toward other minds that can receive them and sustain them.

Recognizing that this porous tendency is natural to the human being, one must develop more than human fragility. One needs to be superphysically aware before he can distinguish spiritual properties. Therefore, strive again and again for stillness needful to awareness until disciplined attention is attained which does not flicker or change the mind's and the Soul's attunement to the Eternal. Should an inspired thought or plan be projected toward a readied soul, he will distinguish and understand its presence. Gradually the full content of inner instruction will be opened to the aware individual through his quiet receptivity, and its many-sided portents will be disclosed to him. As time continues, each new impulse sent from a Higher Intelligence to a human being will be instantly recognized. Yet always the discipline at the human level must include not only intuitional alertness and responsiveness, but also quietness for expanded and quickened reception.

THIS IS A DAY for hourly attunements. To be successful, an integrated use of all of your faculties is vital. Faulty attunement usually results from too purely mental conceptions, or is due to the energies of the bodies not being lifted in conscious aspiration, or it is caused by insufficient interest. It is

18

of greatest importance that you practice realizing complete stillness from the center of yourself. *Stillness must be controlled.* When controlled, the feelings and mind and Soul forms can contribute their particular energies toward the establishment of ever-improving identification with higher states of being.

IN the morning period, recall your individual requirements—both spiritual and practical—and enable them to be manifested into being through your at-one-ing with their archetypal source. Let this period include prayers for others.

At high noon devote yourself entirely to world prayer. Individualize and globalize your attunement to the reception of spiritual currents that are broadcast by the sun. When once your reception in each vehicle of consciousness has been received, you shall then attune your nation, the North American continent, and the South American continent to solar baptisms. All continents and islands west of your own nation, and its northern and southern neighbors, shall then be included, after which the European, the African, and other continents will be remembered in that order.

It is within your power to ask that the Supreme Spirit functioning through the Solar Logos ray out to each of these remembered persons and nations Its Light of that frequency which prohibits war.

19

In your evening work, review the day. Idealize this incarnation by endeavoring to realize its possibilities and your unfolding capabilities. Bless the spirit of the family as well as all the atoms of the entire home. Strengthen for seconds or minutes at a time your reception of that Light frequency which prohibits war. Summon and receive this current for the purifying and the acceleration of the home aura. Thirdly, remind yourself that although you are an earthian to all outward appearances, you are also God's son or God's daughter actually, and this world is not your home. Your own dwelling place is the world of Light—that world which is shoreless, timeless and eternal. Through identification with your own kingdom you will invite empowerments from that kingdom.

FOR those who seek unfoldment of the channelship of spiritual healing, the foremost need is to focus one's whole mind on the goal of inward peace. When this assignment is pursued with the vigor and wholeheartedness which is deemed necessary, then will your conscious channeling of healing resources begin.

The second step for the disciple to take toward the change of his mental life is related to the overcoming of negative thoughts.

Just as you would no longer take into your body food whose effect is poisonous and destroying, so must you reject deliberately all unsavory and unpleasant thoughts from your continued attention.

Your goal is a mind centered in the fountain of everlasting spiritual renewal. Therefore, you must practice at odd and various periods of your day, as frequently as possible, your mind's cleansing. Envision streams of sparkling, purifying, anointing God Light as bathing the contents of your bodies, your aura, and your emanations in this moment of resolute pause. The purpose of the mind's entire contents receiving purification, enlivening and enlightening must be held before the inner self with objectivity.

Thirdly, a great lack in far too many pupils is the failure to use good picturization or imagery. Following the mind's cleansing, the field of your consciousness should be sown with God Incentives. Let yourself be interested in the envisionment of a world constantly at peace, of active brotherhood among men, of human beings' openness and receptivity to the forces of spiritual renewal. Always beginning with life nearest at hand, you should see the world near and around you as reflective of world peace, of progressiveness, and of spiritual openness to the highest truths.

At this particular point in your deliberations you should call to mind, with the intention of goodwill, the blessing of groups, causes or individuals you happen at the moment to remember. Although we are describing what needs to be done as a new life habit which is to become permanent, it is not our meaning to imply that you can carry out these suggestions in a single period. Rather are they to be distributed into the different portions of your day and night. You must be interested and faithful in the cleansing of your thoughts. The need of empathy for the world and for the experiences of others should be as natural to remembrance as are mealtimes and times of retirement and awakenment.

Fourthly, while driving a car there should always be times of silent work done for others. Regardless as to how many may be riding with you, any drive in a motor vehicle should start with your invocation for Divine protection first, and then you should follow the protective work with the thought: *"Supreme God of the Highest Resources of Divinity, let these moments, as well as my thoughts, be channels for the outflow of benefic currents into humanity, into world government, and into all the systems and movements that are related to the progress of mankind and the creatures. As my thoughts are now with those in need or with those who possess special merit, let Thy spiritual powers streaming through these interests channel new incentives, healing and improvement into these persons."*

One by one, individuals who especially appeal to you at this moment shall be thought of highly and spiritually. As this new persistence of the mind is cultivated and maintained, each one will become aligned to the Spirit of Grace. For the moments you are remembering these persons or causes or needs, they are brought into contact with the Spirit of Grace and Its boundless mercies.

When you are completely interested and possessed by a love of the good, the blessed, and the evolving currents of Divinity, you will find yourself healed and made centered in wholeness which is the good you seek. Be busy exercising your mental faculties with all the diligence you contain.

IN your evening walk, after your attunement to the Lord Christ, call His name several times; after which you may more easily find your consciousness resting in gathered and maintained peace. It is from the pool of this peace that spiritual thoughts can radiate into you. It will be necessary for you to listen inwardly and creatively, if for only a word or a phrase.

Continue to remember all of your Elder Brothers and Sisters who, because of Christ, are enfolding your planet with dynamic wavelengths. Be at peace, for only thus can your day be attuned and beautiful.

GRACE be unto you through Christ. It is time to acquaint you with essential devotions, practices and overcomings necessary for bridging communions between earth and heaven.

Our special duty and our supreme joy is to acquaint you more thoroughly with our Elder Brother Who bears the title and is the officiant known as Christ. Today we are sending legions of Light through the earth urging persons individually and unitedly to become centers of peace—*centers of alignment for Christ to use. Whenever you are prone to respond to haste, impatience or anger you are delaying the conquest of earth by the hosts who worship God.* You also curtain earth and prevent the door of world peace from opening by permitting yourself to experience separation in feeling or thought from any living person, creature or thing.

You are urged especially to bring to peace your entire life in addition to all of the interests with which you are associated and all of the energies which charge you. *Allow yourself no liberties in expressing anything whatsoever which closes out the Light. Know that every individual, animal, instrument and event you encounter, or with which you must be associated, should be allowed to enter your attention peacefully, your thoughts courteously, your employment and care lovingly.* How can Christ ordain or make possible the era of peace until you, and others like you who realize communication with Light, are unbroken mirrors of that true Light? You should never permit any indulgence of anger at yourself or of shame regarding yourself. Let there be peace, reverence and certainty of that kind which attunes you with kingdoms and levels and orders of supernal peace! *Cease to serve death by conquering in yourself all that separates, distorts or censures.* In your own heart lift up every offender, every imperfect instrument, every troubled situation, until the Light in your innermost sanctuary blesses, renews and transforms completely the elementals composing your body and your instruments of action.

The Christ Hierarchy is closer to you than you know and much more concentrated upon you and the details of your living and serving than you have ever realized. From this time forward, serve Christ in peace. Endeavor to make beautiful, complete and gracious all that you think or attempt while under the observation of the Wise and the Strong.

In this moment you have only to do or to fulfill the qualifications of discipleship; the training of the golden now will be elongated into that inner growth toward which you are being pointed.

May that Light which never fades and the song of inner gladness which sings forever, live immortally in your heart and being.

KEYS TO CREATIVE MEDITATION

*Meditation is an open door into the wide
spaces of powers you can touch only when
in direct contact with them.*

BECAUSE meditation is of such intrinsic value in
your becoming, our words to you this day are
addressed toward your improvement in these inner
ways. Prayer work based on hourly rhythms has
both strengthening and penetrating benefits. We
suggest, therefore, that you practice remembrance
of the inner worlds on the even hours of your day.
Better realization and depth work can be accomplished if you have a good program to follow on
each of these rhythmic timings. Henceforth, *let
your remembrance include the daily climbing of
your Jacob's ladder.* These as you might imagine,
are steps in daily contemplation of your upward
strivings.

Every aspirant should consider, after the exercise of the alignment technique, his incarnation's
delineation of the ladder. Some of these steps will
include considerations of personal significance.

Be sure to allow for these united realizations:
First, spiritual purposefulness. The second step of
the individual Jacob's ladder should be the prac-

tice of increased reverence for this day. The self-explanatory phases of these steps are quite obvious and need no further description. The third step should be improvement in the recognition and use of spiritual realities and laws applicable to the day.

The fourth step of this ladder of consideration is *responsibility* as in regard to individual knowledge of esoteric actualities. We shall here explain that at this step each aspirant needs to review, basically and vitally, his chief interests in knowledge herein shared and to which he responds most deeply. Let these include a consideration of the great Brotherhood of Perfected Souls and their relation to humanity's progress.

On one of the foregoing steps which pertains to the use of spiritual dynamics, one should each day round out and strive to perfect the treatment work. Other steps than these which we have given will come as individual recognitions of the steps to be taken in this incarnation, such as steps in greater self-control, self-mastery, or toward enlightenment.

On one of the days of the week, at two-hour intervals after the *first* meditation period which will include a brief review of the Jacob's ladder, begin in the *second* period of remembrance with an attunement with the great centers of power in the inner kingdoms. One of the first contacts with these actual centers would be that of *Shamballa*. One by one throughout the day other great centers would be remembered during subsequent rhythmic meditation periods.

The *third* remembrance period in the day will consist of attunement to that great heaven known as *Nirvana.*

The *fourth* heavenly center's attunement will be that of *Elysium;* and in the *fifth* period of remembrance you will attune yourself to *Arcadia.*

The last center to be remembered in the next period will be that of a new power broadcast—one which we call *Ebrilium* (ee BRILL ee um). It is a most highly developed center of administration and realization on the Fifth Ray (the Ray of Science), and one that is entered only after advanced enlightenment.

Again, the center of powerful broadcast on the Sixth Ray is that of *Paradise;* and on the Seventh is that of *Olympus.* Each of these centers radiates its own unique and energetic velocities. These specialized centers are responsible for the perfecting of all endeavors synonymous with these places. For instance, Shamballa is interrelated with government; the center Nirvana with the radiation of Divine Peace; Elysium with the attainment of perfect or completed understanding. Another phrase which signifies this center is that of Divine Wisdom and its broadcast.

The fourth, Arcadia, is the center where all creative endeavor exists in ideal prototypes, and is as well the feeding ground or the center of containment for all creative arts and their spiritualizations.

In Ebrilium, a center of tremendous force, are the ideas, archetypes and powers which possess all gathered information in regard to science in its diversified phases.

In Paradise are the living forms of all which religion teaches and symbolizes. Since many of you function upon this ray, your recognition of Paradise should be stronger than of the other centers, at least in your inaugural attunements.

In Olympus are great monumental rituals whose powers are unbrokenly being wielded through its ray. Consider, exercise and develop realization concerning these new commitments.

Maintain and be centered in that point within you which holds God.

PERSISTENCE becomes the disciple. Its fruits are faith's results. From within, your attention to details, your application of principles, and your long range vision are momently observed and carefully recorded always. It is important to be diligent in the mellowing of character and in giving permission to God's energies of quickening which will not only cleanse you completely, but accomplish an inner preparation at the same time for the higher life of persistent discipleship.

In preparing for meditation, these are the simple

but requisite states needful to your conquest: Ere meditation begins, mentally take a journey into the higher ranges of consciousness by attentively remembering to enter all the gates which lead to direct at-one-ment.

The first gate is the one of *Purification*. Here you will pause to exercise a shedding of non-essentials and low-grade qualities and forces. Not until all these powers belonging to the world have been consciously shed can you approach with worthiness the second gate—*The Gate of Preparation*.

Within the new area there needs to be practiced a jurisdiction over harmonizing, sweetening, gentling and worshiping qualities. All these aspects of the higher nature should be so wielded that their emanation is recognized at the outer rim of consciousness as well as the center. When fully receptive to the incoming and the harmonizing velocities of Spirit, the third gate may be approached.

This is the gate called *Faith's Understanding*. In this region of consciousness one aspires to equip himself more thoroughly with the enforcements of known information—revealed by teaching, intuition or empirical understanding. Allow the mind to summarize the elements of mental focus that pertain to the day's requirements. Review this department of consciousness with deliberate and searching care in freer times so that your selectivity of working forces, of spiritual implements of use

31

are well considered. In days of activity, brief selections of remembered counsel, teaching and idealism will be possible.

The fourth gate is the *Gate of Realization.* In the mystic's terminology it could also be called the "Gate of Contemplation." Here you deal with a wider and more expansive remembrance of spiritual realities. *The mind needs to be set free in this domain so that it can spontaneously choose certain aspects for reflection,* for it may travel over mountainous peaks of spiritual understanding, gaining spiritual delight through its survey. Usually within this field lie ideals rather than attained qualities. Here dwell the futurity energies that need contact with the thinker in order to be linked with his orbit.

Beyond this gate is the gate on which is emblazoned the brightest Light, for here, through the *Gate of Direct Communion,* one passes into the experience of the worship of the Presence.

Consider these gates and move through them with practiced skill. Divine Peace shall light your path.

IN THE COURSE of spiritual instruction it is often wise to explore new meditative practices over a period of several weeks. Such is the intent of this direction. Instead of two-hour remembrance intervals, change your rhythm to one which practices remembrance every four hours beginning at nine o'clock and followed by one o'clock, and finally by your remembrance at five o'clock. The manner in which you shall conduct these remembrances is of the type which necessitates slower, more thorough and more self-giving devotion to the Highest. You will spend no less than fifteen minutes in each of these periods and you are urged to meditate upon the realities of the great God Presence and Its surrounding Presences. For example, you might begin on a certain day, in your period devoted to peace, with your expression of worship for God Immanent. This could be followed at one o'clock by your invocation, in the name of the Lord Emmanuel, to the mighty Logos of Peace for His attunement and enfoldment of man on earth. At five o'clock you would remember the Elohim which serve God Immanent.

On another day you would devote three periods to depth meditation upon the three Great Ones—the Lord of Life, sometimes called the Manu; the Lord of Regeneration for the planet, the Christ; and the Lord known as Maha Chohan, the dispenser of spiritual truth.

Later, attention may focus upon the Hierarchy; and finally the Angel Orders may be included, always beginning with their Kings and Princes and taking up by regular degrees each of the main divisions of the Angelic Kingdom as revealed in a previous series of instructions.*

With each remembrance of these outstanding Servers, be self-giving, self-releasing in worship of the Good which exercises itself through these who are most responsible for man's enlightenment.

SINCE it is needful that you come to larger harvests, you must learn to accelerate the wavelengths by which these new powers and benefits may reach you and be born in you. For that reason you are asked to concentrate in daily meditations upon new relationships. This pertains to your building up an association through desire at first, and then through the adventure of meeting new persons and the making of new adjustments that will advance you into new efforts in self-development and in your at-one-ment with the infinities and possibilities of the Eternal Realm. So you are given simply this key and cue: Dwell creatively upon establishing new relationships, first through desire, and then through growth, and at last through eased attainment.

On another day your key and cue will be to break the bonds of the old by expanding your confinements, by overcoming fixed thoughts and habits until you are conscious of the germs of new leadings, tendencies and ideals.

*See, *The Kingdom of the Shining Ones*

On a third day meditate upon newness in an inclusive sense, a newness of directed and inspired plans being born in the minds of willing recipients on earth from the source of the Hierarchy. Meditate upon newness not only blessing and enfolding your whole earth in ways of progressive thought and effort but consider the new frequencies, presences and treasures of spirit that your whole earth may discover spiritually. With all of these meditations pay special heed to your most vital keys of interest. Be certain to make note of them.

On yet a fourth day, meditate insightfully upon yourself with newness of idealization, resolve and enthusiasm. It is very helpful to gain a detached perspective of oneself, and to tread a thread-like path toward a new horizon. Gradually that thread-like impression of the real in you will open out into a well traveled path of consistent and continuous practice.

On a final day, become familiar with the promptings, yearnings and preferences of your real self. Rest in them. Be joyful in their recognition. On the following week you will carry over the unfinished work of this week's glimpses. You will strive more ardently, intelligently and consistently to open up to newness, to attract the inevitable, but henceforth in the *now*. You will make friends with the distant. The familiar and the ever-present are all too close to you so that you are engulfed by it and your perspective is dimmed. In order to encourage futurity powers and realizations, we want you to quicken the buds of highest longings of your Soul through dedicated interest. For that reason, welcome and receive benedictions of newness.

RARELY do disciples experience the *horizon consciousness*. That you may use it, we shall explain it as simply as possible. In a later lesson, after your own practice and experimentation, we shall elucidate more strongly the meanings.

Restfulness and inspiredness cause all the faculties of being to turn their focus upon higher levels of objectives. When the mental body is highly motivated and is most energetic, then it achieves the periphery of consciousness which exists between the causative and the mental worlds. Ordinarily some portion or fraction of consciousness is burdened by low-grade encumbrances. But on these rare occasions each faculty voluntarily lifts to its highest level of acceleration and this periphery which is all important to man's fullest development is achieved.

At the beginning of the causative world exist those archetypes which are ready for future experience. They are the ones which by conscious or unconscious invitation have achieved full-blown enlargement and have become the completed designs which are necessary for the inducement of physical manifestation. Usually months and sometimes years are required for the radiations from the archetypes to mingle ideally with the next lower dimensions.

In the person possessing faith, vertical consciousness is expressive. Chiefly by faith's means in these highlighted periods, the periphery which contains man's future is entered and known. By this means, through the energies of faith's ascent, that level is touched which was, the moment beforehand, designated as the future. *Now that future is known through the causative world's intuitional consciousness—the future has already descended and been made a part of the active present.*

These attitudes of consciousness and endeavor are not understood easily. It will be needful that you study, sentence by sentence, all of the instruction that is given you regarding the *horizon consciousness.*

The goal for each disciple and pupil is the attainment of that energized and uplifted vertical attitude which will bring each aspirant into recognized contact with the realm in which his best good awaits releasement. A high degree of expectancy, reverent interest in the purposes of existence, and faith's energizing, together form the springboard for this achievement of the *causative consciousness.* It is the realization of what is stored in this region which forms the basis of prophecy, invention and individual progress.

Realize then that the *horizon consciousness* contains a world of realities that are functioning for your advancement beyond your loftiest dreaming. The time will come when you will be able to keep your vertical consciousness so alive, instructive and energetic that your spiritual perception will realize a wide reach in God attunement through the *immensity consciousness*. Then you will not be thinking of a place on earth where your physical body is located, but of spacelessness charged with Light. Your consciousness all the while will act in a circular manner to inform you of the fertility as well as the width and height and depth of your spiritual arc within the center of your God circle, for that is what this workable field is. You should then be more conscious of the fruits of Spirit.

Now it should begin to dawn upon you why you are being initiated into the new interests of regions beyond your usual thoughts. You still require improvement in your creative interest in *meditation*. To most of you it is a duty, something that is required to be done and borne—perhaps with difficulty. Remember, meditation is an open door into the wide spaces of powers you can touch only when in direct contact with them. Do not expect or require your perfection, at least not now in these beginning disciplines. Nevertheless you are urged to make a better than your best effort in order that you succeed in breaking the crystalization of old habits.

ALLOW your thoughts to move forward through the hours from morning until night, gaining a wide sweep of the expectations of your better handling of them in this day. It is very needful for everyone who is inclined to extreme idealism, dreaminess, or unwholesome introversion to come to the conquest of these deficiencies. It is just as needful for those who are ineffectual to become at last effectual as it is for the unloving to become compassionate, mercy giving, and genuinely out giving of themselves to others.

Certain requirements for the growth of individuals in these meditative periods need to be mentioned. The impetuous person, in his prayer times, needs to concentrate upon peace, serenity, and the deliberate tranquilizing of his emotions and his reactions. The light of his new and deliberate self-control will thoughtfully affect his conduct, softening, enriching, blessing and harmonizing it until he can live at peace within himself.

Let the nervous, excitable individuals be the ones chiefly to pray for peace, harmony and serenity in the conduct and affairs of men. The power they generate while praying for others will help to bring about their own healing.

Let those who speak too much and waste their effort in needless talkativeness be those who pray for illumination and for all the gifts that come from self-command, the resolute quieting of non-essentials or the conquest of those instincts which lead to acts that are inconsequential.

IN THE EVENINGS at the hour of six o'clock, you are to recall thoughtfully your citizenship with Eternity in prayerful words like these: *"I am a Soul who has taken on the cloak of mortality. In my true selfhood I am free. I am invested with capabilities and powers that belong to Godhood. I am a citizen of that experience which includes all the good creations of Divinity. I am at a level now in my remembrance with the Angels and the Iofel and the Tuma—the great, consciously evolving sisters and brothers of other Orders of Beings. From this world, from this limitlessness of energy, beauty and creativity, I draw new, glowing embers of remembrance. May this recollection of my true selfhood and identification with the Eternity from which I originate lend power and significance and mastery to my finite existence."*

THE ATOMIC TREATMENT

*He who is able to govern the atoms of any
particular region is able to govern life.*

ONE of the points of first importance concerns
your learning to *practice the government of
your own selfhood.* Each one of your bodies—the
Soul, mental, emotional, etheric and physical—possesses trillions of elemental or atomic intelligences.
The higher the energy, the loftier the evolution
of these atomic intelligences. It is needful that
from your Soul Self you begin to become aware of
the millions of elemental lives constituting your
Soul's body. Learn to bless them with goodwill.
Such a blessing shall contain faith in their ultimate
upliftment and progress. Then, keeping wholly
conscious control, *learn henceforth to cause your
mental body's atoms to face upward; and like an
older brother or sister, feel your Soul's pure Light
acknowledging and shining upon every atomic
form constituting your mental body.* Give orders
in love and hope for your mental faculty to work
peacefully and receptively in service to the Light
of Spirit. Survey your mental body intuitively realizing your need for improved memory, expanded
knowledge, and accelerated intelligence.

In the same manner, from your Soul's awareness again shine the Light of Spirit upon and into every atomic life which constitutes your emotional vehicle. In each of you it is this form which is the most unruly and likely to be most disobedient to Spirit. Lovingly and prayerfully, with the consciousness of blessing, remember the atomic lives within this emotional faculty—this body in which most of you enter the inner worlds at night. Spiritually command this form to cease its childishness and all responses to instinctive emotions. *Give the atoms of your emotional form a hunger for the serenity that comes only from responsiveness to that which is beautiful and ennobling.*

Next, focus the Light which flows from the Spirit and illumines the Soul, upon the nebulous form—your etheric vehicle. Of all your members it is the most easily disturbed and the most readily influenced. Lovingly the Soul shall look upon the etheric body, envisioning it mentally. Were you gifted with inner sight, at first glance you would notice whirling forces of light rose energy whose currents point downward. It requires concerted effort of one-pointed concentration to bless reverently the trillions of atomic intelligences composing this vehicle. Being highly responsive, etheric atoms turn quickly to an influence of Light. As your Soul has communion with the responsive atoms it must learn by practice to reverently com-

mand the atoms to cause their whirls of energy to
move upward. This should precipitate a reaction
of body lightness and more quickly unite the atoms
with the sources of their renewal. At these times
*intone the blue spirit of prana so that new life will
be called into activity by this special energy.*

Prana itself has an indefinite, silver grey quality
in the etheric world, but in the astral world its emanation is a purplish blue. It is this prana that is
needed to restore the etheric atoms and to endow
them with vitality that is unfailing.

A serious change of tempo on your part, such as
an alteration of mood from that of joyousness and
veneration to one of aggressive impatience, causes
these atoms to cease radiating energy in the outgoing sense. Such impacts of lower power and attitudes cause them to follow the direction of the energies that are sweeping through the aura. In this
type of event, hurry and aggressiveness cause the
atomic intelligences to focus their whirls of power
downward. This is not the position in which they
are able to be revitalized. The upward arc of their
flowing energies must consciously be achieved ere
a resurgence and maintenance of energy is gained.

In the same manner *direct God Light from the
Spirit Indwelling, through the Soul's command
and attention, into the physical form.* The chakra
most readily accelerated by this attention is the
third one, known as the subconscious brain of the

body. It is the third chakra in the physical body that is the medium by which the reception of vitality flows either downward or circulates evenly in upward movements throughout the whole physical organism. You must learn to speak with loving firmness to the unconscious member or subconscious brain in such a way that you will win its instantaneous obedience.

Beginning with your head region, reflect upon the countless thousands of atoms constituting your head, both the bone structure and its inner matter. Move the Light upon the throat; center it there. Speak to the intelligences forming the skin and the inner organs. Knowing the various components of this body mechanism, call the members in any one area of your physical form by name. If there is thyroid abnormality, address the atoms composing this organ urging them to return in expression and potency to their archetypal vitality, to carry out constructively the design of their Supreme Creator. Then moving slowly throughout the entire body, concentrate upon various areas including the right and left sides, giving separate attention to each of these divisions of the body. For instance, revitalize the atoms of the lungs by singling them out and by directing them to come into the complete expression of their Maker's pattern for them.

In each of these areas you will find that if you have a weakness in any of them, your interest and

*your benediction of the atomic universe composing
each of your vehicles will glow with a warm agreement.* Or it might be said that the stimuli it receives cause it to feel warm in contrast to the rest
of your being. Center a great deal of attention upon those parts or organs which are faulty. It is well
to urge the subconscious brain throughout all the
hours and all the years of your life to give watchful
assistance to that region. To the organ itself your
message can vary each day, but its substance must
contain the Divine command to measure up in radiation and fulfillment of expression to perfect
functioning in accordance with its purpose.

Treat the atoms in your remembrance times and
call upon them to vibrate agelessness, for it is possible for them to be endowed through their own
receptivity with solar stimuli motivating them
from the central Self within.

IMPRESS the atoms of each of your bodies with
the imprint of all the power that will make them
express perfection. The outer band of each atom
is called the *orium band*. It is this influential band,
magnetically surrounding each atom, which is the
attracting life force.

In your physical forms, should there be a tendency to be over-emotional, the orium circle will
be affinitized to water or fluids and will hold them
in the physical body. If you are the opposite, high-

ly mental and unemotional your orium ring will repel those normal fluidic powers from filling your body with needful fluids. Energize this outer rim of each atom with wise magnetizing.

REMEMBER, with reference to the work of the atomic intelligences, he who is able to govern the atoms of any particular region is able to govern life. Mastership consists of the pure and attained conquest of every atomic body with which one has to deal.

We have mentioned that every atom is banded by three electrical rings. Only when these bands are functioning in rhythm and at the same rate of speed does the intelligence within the atom stir and affect its whole miniature world.

The inner ring, which in our threshold we name the *edam band, actually consists of the memory of nature as it pertains to each organism used.* Every physical body you have ever worn has been made up of atoms whose inner rings recorded, according to each vehicle's way, stored impressions of your pilgrimage. In order for you to be released from every negative influence that besets you, as carried over from your past, you must by yourselves be able to keep the edam band within the atoms active in accumulating constructive impressions. In time these shall feed the whole atom and all its nuclei with their gladdening and positive energies. *It shall be by the strength of these wholesome forces deliberately chosen by man's conscious decisions that these latent carriers of negatives will in time be purified and raised up into new activations of naturally constructive powers.* Then when this occurs one whose edam rings are so treated shall cease to be influenced by any force of the past or by any repetition of its memories.

The middle band which we call the *poreas ring* is the one with which you must deal the most carefully. *Should this band, due to improper thinking, feeling or living, become disturbed and its rhythm broken, it may either move counterclockwise or its pattern may become feeble.* Moreover, when treated carelessly it shall be the means by which the entire atom and its radiating centers begin the deterioration or decay which invites disease and which causes a gradual cessation of their lives. This middle band, the poreas ring, holds that which affects the shape of your physical bodies. Indeed, it is constantly discharging energies which impregnate the hereditary genes within a physical body. When very active, the physical inheritances from the individual thus activated will be strong and definite. This band is influencing, even at this moment, that which you will further unfold in relation to stored inheritance factors from those who have constituted your family tree.

47

Parents who fail to impress their children with any of their likenesses lack genes of vigor. This in turn is caused by a poorly rotating and a somewhat weakened poreas ring.

If this band can be impressed and cleansed from all friction, all poor functioning, all weakened effort, if it can be motivated to positive recordings and impartings of its own forces, your present functioning will attune you to forces of health; and what you might receive of physical disease unknowingly handed down to you by your ancestors, will not come to pass. You can instead receive from this ring only that which will maintain good life, strong vitality, and the best of your family's inheritance factors.

The third and outermost rim which is called the *orium ring* does not refer to a color; it refers rather to the quality of forces which this particular rim circulates. The orium ring is a radiant band revolving around every atom's world. Like a physical sun, it moves at tremendous speeds and as it moves it gives life. *It broadcasts and radiates the potencies released by the entire atom throughout the whole of the particular vehicle in which it is active.*

Should atoms in the physical foot be physically injured, all three bands would be affected. The third ring, however, would be particularly and noticeably handicapped by its slow rhythm and its inability to pour out its electrical energies into the field of its radiating center.

The orium band is peculiar in that its mission consists of bringing up from the center of the atom and broadcasting abroad electrical chargings that give life to the body. Furthermore, according to its discharges will an individual experience radiant or weakened health. *Since this is the most sensitive of all the bands and the widest in its radiating qualities, it can be consciously impressed and dealt with in every body so that it not only functions at a proper rate of speed for radiant health but it likewise is responsive to your every wish and reverent command for new unfoldments.* This is the rim which holds the power to awaken the whole area of a body or an individual organ to new expressions. It will transform the sick member into health or an aging body into the wholeness of maturity if properly fed and consciously nurtured by constructive forces.

The rims from the atoms are the forces by which the akashic record stores its treasures. When one body, physically speaking, has completed its life, all of the atomic energies gathered by the rings are transferred to the akashic record.

Therein lies your work—in learning better how to command the atomic intelligences to do their work in rhythm, each band aurically encircling the atom carrying its beneficent qualities and discharging heightened electrical energies into the entire auric content of your forms.

After your regular meditation and prayer efforts, invite and welcome the flow of God Light to enter all your vehicles beginning with the God Flame. You are urged to use the word *Adonai* to denote the body which channels and holds the God Light. Next of course, comes your Soul and in this order treat briefly for the cleansing, renewing and strengthening of all of the atoms of your various vehicles. Try to direct the atoms into new patterns of behavior, of expression and of radiance. *Do not work with the electrical bands surrounding these atoms until the end of your treatment for all the vehicles.* Then speak the word for the clearing of these three atomic bands in all your bodies at one time.

A subsequent procedure, which is now needful in order for you to deepen your work in relation to assuming command of your own atomic beings, is this: When you have spoken the directive for the clearing of your three rings, then mention these words: *"And let the flow of Infinite God Light enter the heart of the atom, making it a glowing center—a veritable sun. Let my body, on every plane of expression, be composed of Light which proceeds from innumerable suns within me."*

It is this last treatment which has the greatest

sustaining effect and which accomplishes transformations that are desired.

WOMEN's atoms are more highly attuned to inspirational and intuitive beams because they are feminine and are to be the mothers of the race. Their second rim, the poreas band, is far wider than in the atoms of men. It is the attunement center of each cell. Men are impregnated with power from the Primal Source which gives them life consciousness in this world attuned to the sphere in which they find themselves. Since men are polarized with life force so invincibly, they are conscious predominantly of that world their consciousness occupies. But you are being taught to better polarize your atoms and therefore your bodies, so that all the dimensions shall equally find response.

There is a key word which helps to bring about the polarization of these atomic intelligences. We call it "Elam." To us it signifies Om, or God, but it also has the effect of helping to bring into immediate alignment all of the bodies that have been rightly attuned, centering them in equilibrium.

CENTEREDNESS DURING CRISES

There is nothing you cannot do when the Spirit Indwelling within you is allowed to give Its help.

IN the midst of your spiritual straining, learn to relax. Solemnity in its place is fitting, yet that quality belongs to the Spirit, while rejoicing belongs to all of your vehicles that open responsively to God.

Let your bodies be poised, deliberately relaxing them to such an extent that you feel yourself leaning against the veritable strength of supporting God. Learn to express poised understanding, patient reception, and relaxed conduct. Your minds race—they chase as if pursuing hares that are in themselves inconsequential. To conquer this tension, this mad pursuit of the non-essentials, you have only to remember one word—*poise*. In it lies the possibility of your *oneness with God*.

Follow this exercise if you would be a pupil of discipleship training: When an event tries you, remind yourself, *"This is the instant for relaxed mastery. Now I shall be attuned to that which is real while I observe and consider the outward aspects of this situation."* Should you be late and there is an urgent demand for hurry, let your body be fleet but keep your mind tranquil. It is only when the mind races that you lose your access to invincible power. When one bores you with needless chatter, be attentive, be loving and considerate, but occasionally with quietness of conduct and largeness of thought send forth a silent command, *"Peace, be still,"* or *"Summarize, my friend."*

Learn to conserve your forces through silence when in your automobiles. When with many and while there is action or speed or conversation about you, practice serenity. The mind can soar through the endless heights of Eternity while the body rests in patient mastery during some crisis or in the midst of some interesting events.

Do not be cockatoos, nor swans. You are humans who are being taught to become consciously God-centered. This workmanship of God still needs the Creator's hands in chiseling, that the Divine may have its way with you while you learn above all things *to be still.*

THERE is one particular point imperative to your knowing and practicing. *It is your need to exercise the faculty of spiritual knowing in the midst of unpleasantness, unhappiness, ill health or disaster.* It is needful for you to align yourselves with your own solar consciousness especially faithfully during crises. You must learn to think up to your level of contact with Light power. Having found it, you must gather in through receptivity, through request, and through spiritual breaths or inhalations of energy, all that you can hold. Reason to yourselves at these times: "This is where my power resides. This is my innermost Holy of Holies which none can assail—not any man, nor any draft of ill will. I may invite, and will do so frequently, all whom I love as well as the good things I appreciate into the unfoldment of my remembrance. That which cannot belong in oneness, beauty, power or purpose to the Solar Kingdom shall not receive my attention."

By centering your own recognition upon the assurances and certainties the Soul level has for you, you gather forces for spiritual endurance, for unbroken faith, as well as hope for the positive outcome. By your alignment with the innermost Holy of Holies, a stream of attunement acts as a pathway between your inner world and your world of objective manifestation. Let the promise of destiny and the fortitude of your Soul keep your body and outward circumstances related to the regulations of spiritual command.

Let the Light of Spirit encircle and inhabit you. Be conscious that it is our work to be aware of each pupil's testing and that our watchfulness is over him and all of humanity. Whenever a disciple or devotee promises to be of use to the Hierarchy, his strength will be tried. This we cannot prevent, although we can point the way to conquest.

When evil attacks, there is a numbing sensation and a period of endurance. During the interim of this initial attack, the will forces within the disciple are strengthened and fired. Should you be stunned by the blow of a formidable enemy whose motives are carriers of darkness, bear this in mind:

In order to surmount such foes you will need in these times to posit and empower your will to be stronger for the right than the testing forces. Your success in defending a righteous cause so threatened is dependent upon your ability, agility and intelligence in being *warriors of the Spirit*. Out of successful combat can come your own individual purification of all that is unnecessary, false, vainglorious and impure. During such episodes, it is needful for you to make great inner sacrifices of negative qualities in order to attain the power from within to be impervious to your foes. As soon as every atom and aspect of the endangered situation are permeated by the steadfast consciousness of God Purpose, there will no longer exist fear or exposure to the forces of attack. Such occasions are your own testing for the Cause of Light, and from our own experience we can knowingly counsel that the battle is hard but the victory is enduring and splendid.

It is then that you must be bold, confident, calm

and trusting—bold to protect your rights, confident that Light is superior to darkness; and you must be unafraid in the midst of the battle.

Do not imagine for a moment that whenever attacked, your position is too imperiled. Your enemies are apt to act quickly in order to wrest from you the prize or advantage desired while you are stunned. You must always have the equal of their cunning and their avarice, only your weapons must be those of sharpened spiritual faculties and qualities.

Do not act disturbed or fearful during such times. Instead, reveal a fighting spirit. Your warriorship is of and for the Light and you can be successful only if you are undaunted and unafraid and spiritually fortified on each level of existence.

From our side, there are only Light and volumes of power for all of your emergencies. Cause the Light to descend and to enter your need and to channel your thoughts and your activities on these occasions. Above all, do not underestimate or overestimate an enemy. Consider your resources and see them as your protection. Lift your head and your heart to the Light and be aware that you are companioned and safefolded by Those who love you and trust you to prove yourself valiantly capable of defending any righteous Cause.

IT IS ADVISABLE that at regular intervals you call

upon the White Armies of Christ to attack the dark psychic cesspools close to the physical plane. We desire that you remember that there are legions and legions of pure Souls whose work is peace. We want you to be a discoverer yourself of the un-numbered hosts dedicated to the protection and the salvation of humanity. You can meet these Armies of the Light in your own positive and valorous ef-forts. Call them into the earth's atmosphere. Di-rect them to certain areas which you know of as in need of attention this day. Repeat, *"O Mighty One, let me be joined to those ranks of servers who scatter the darkness and bring forth the Light."*

THE CONTAINMENT OF GOD INBEING

There is in each of you a heaven you are not touching—a place of monumental powers.

FROM the heights of the Hierarchy let your Souls know peace, let your minds be bathed in spiritual purity, and let the whole consciousness be turned to God.

Now it is our intention to speak to you of the greatest reality you each contain. What we tell you is to become the basis of meditative work you will use in your inaugural treatment period for each new day. This is the most important inner work with which you shall be occupied.

The threshold of God is within you and you possess containment of God *Inbeing*. Instead of recognizing the holy innermost Presence as something vague and undefined, you must come to a stronger at-one-ment with Indwelling Divinity. After your alignment technique* is exercised each morning, you will pronounce the phrase *God Inbeing* after the intonement of the Trinity Powers. In coming to this realization of the important reality of God Inbeing in you, you will need to pause at the entrance to this actuality and be in active communion with Divinity Innermost.

*See, *Gateways Into Light*

How will you sense God Within? First, you must practice the strong awareness of reverent recognition. Secondly, in veneration you must, through desire and aspiration, pray before the altar of God Inbeing. In your realization be certain to keep your consciousness rightly focused. You will place yourself in the position you now are in as looking up to the Divine Light Presence which penetrates you. Seated naturally in meditation, you will sense God Presence as your Holy of Holies Indwelling— as the Self of Light which completely enfolds you, easily and deeply in whatever position you assume. Do not imagine this God Self to be in any area apart or distinct from you. It, in Divinity, will follow the natural outlines of your own body positions.

Thirdly, speak to your God Self with new veneration and inclusion each day. Your words should approximately follow this outline: *"O God Inbeing, holy and wise art Thou. Send into all of me the raying of Thy Light, the blessing of Thy Spirit, the transforming of Thy Power. Help me to become conscious of Thee forevermore, and to channel forth Thy Mysteries in quietness and in reverence. Through Thy holy Presence Indwelling, thus shall it be."*

Fourthly, each new day you will spend a few minutes in creative contemplation of God in your being. On one day you will remember that this

God Flame, composed of individual form, is a complete replica in power, intelligence and divinity of God the Whole. Through the means of God Inbeing the whole of Divinity blesses, inspires and enlightens you.

Fifthly, now the raying through of individual Deity's Light needs to be directed to the regeneration and the perfecting of beinghood. This refers to the spiritualizing, the governing, and the uplifting of the velocities or the states of vibration of every vehicle belonging to the total being. To accomplish this you will wait, through one-pointed desire, upon the benedictions of God Inbeing energizing all of Its vehicles of expression from the Adonai downwards. In this invocation of benediction from God Indwelling you must desire, as each body is remembered, Deity's fullest penetration and healing of the faculty of the vehicle considered.

Not in one meditation, but in such a time as a day's rhythmic remembrances you would consider God Inbeing's acceleration of the life current. In your second treatment period of the day you would begin with the vehicle of individuality or Adonai, asking God Inbeing in you consciously to bless the whole faculty of individualized will. This faculty may have been weak. You will remember to ask for a greater degree of will empowerment.

With the faculty of Soul you will ask that there be strengthening and an appointing of Soul gifts or

61

energies which need special consideration at the time of treatment. For instance, if your intuitional qualities are too dim, and if you feel that they may be unreliable, in one particular morning's work you will ask for empowerment of true and God-given realizations of reality.

On another day it might possibly be the faculty of creativity which is perceivably weak. Thus the increase of the fires of creativity will be sought through the blessing of God Inbeing.

From the mental world earthward it is well at least once each week to treat specifically for health to ray out and through from God Inbeing. (With the pronouncement of the words, *God Inbeing*, you are to intone your individualized beam of the Living Presence, knowing that it is your individualized Godhead expressing, living and directing all of Its faculties which compose you.) At this place in your treatment work you will ask for God's health through your individualized ray of God to become your vigorous and your full endowment of health on the mental plane. Here you will treat in specific ways for the improvement of discernment, deduction, cognition, memory, and similar mental powers.

Still accenting the theme of health, on the astral level you will state your desire for the health of God Inbeing to reflect through to your emotional body. Quietly, slowly and thoroughly you will realize, raying out and into the body treated, those unique and capable qualities which will harmonize, refine, purify, strengthen and enrich astral capabilities.

In comparable ways the broadcast of cleansing, renewing, health-giving currents into the etheric vehicle will also be accomplished. Here the qualification of contained and insulated energies will be highlighted.

One whole treatment period should be allotted for God Inbeings raying through to the physical channel Its splendid, unvarying health stimuli. Whenever known organs require perfecting, in a most relaxed manner you will let the stimuli from God Inbeing, which has more than x-ray ability, to penetrate the organ placed attentively before Divinity's Presence. Thus you would say:

"God Inbeing, let your Light empowerments ray through to my lungs, . . . to my heart, . . . (or) to my throat."

Be sure to use the personal pronoun "my" in your healing treatments for yourself. These must not be superficial, quick flashing remembrances. You must be slow, deliberate, and fully in reverent attunement with God-in-you.

In ways like these you can approach the grounding of immanent God Presence and God Powers in those matters which are difficult for you, such as social relationships, business appointments, or in

crises. Invite, greet, trust and honor the splendid
Self of God which is in you.

GOD INBEING is made of the substance of Light—
the Light of God. It consists of the equivalents of
intelligence, will, love and motion.

That part of your inner God's Intelligence becomes by reflection your own individual world of
mind. That quality called love, which is an intrinsic aspect of your inner Godhood, reflected downward becomes the world of feeling. Know, therefore, that within your God Indwelling is a composite of all the qualities which are constructive and
which comprise distinct characteristics in the lower levels of God Inbeing's reflections. For that reason, henceforth when your mind needs clarification or stimulus, say to yourself, *"God Inbeing
Within now rays out Its intelligence into every
part of Its selfhood."* Let the mind respond to Its
impulses.

Should the astral body's condition be negative,
you will say, *"God Inbeing Within sends out Its
love, harmony and peace into all the reflections of
my individual being. Let my feelings be trans-
formed and regenerated through the outshining of
Divinity's accelerations."*

The God Self cannot assume government of Its
reflected aspects until the lower forms are quickened by the desire for overshadowing of this kind,

and the life which was present but unfelt becomes the controlling and empowering influence. Only perfected consciousness of the nature of Masterhood and Divine Sonship realizes the fully enthroned power, consciousness and life which your own God Inbeing possesses. No force or intelligence is as near or as immediately effective as your individual God. When in the throes of testing, or on the crest of great emotion, recollect that the Divinity which is enshrined in your innermost center is the most available and answerable for your immediate, urgent needs.

Do not think of your God Indwelling as a wraith or merely as a flame of vague proportions. In size, your individual aspect of God is larger and quite understandably more luminous than any vehicle known to you of your own individual order. This God Spirit dwells forever in the Kingdom of Divinity's Light. Never for one moment has It experienced separation from the Source of Its own origin.

All that you are is the result of the Indwelling God's feeble or well intentioned interests in expansiveness and extensiveness of individual progress. Poor bodies, inadequate living or serving are frequently due to the God Inbeing's lack of interest in the outermost conditions of life. For that reason, in your daily worship it is of paramount importance to remind your individual God—or call it God Spirit, if you will—of all the interests and experiences you, the thinker, wish It to include, enliven and govern. Therefore, practice identification with your God Inbeing.

Secondly, in spiritual patience await and consciously receive the benefits of Its overshadowing.

Thirdly, invite and receive the quickening influences which flow from the experience known occultly as the Great Outshining. It is in this third state that the government of God Indwelling becomes a realized aspect of your own selfhood.

Recall frequently in meditations how God Inbeing is of Logos potential and how It has affiliations with every developed or completed Logos of the Kingdom. On Its infinite network are the prime Logi whose thoughts, shall we say, and sacraments of love continually surround your private shores of Godhood with Their tides. Therefore, to commune with the vibratory benefits of the Solar Logos in charge of our own galactic system, or the Logos presiding over all known island universes, brings through such power to you. To receive quickenings of the sun spiritually, you would need to begin your affiliation with like energies through the bridge of contact in your God Self. Should this God Inbeing Self be unawakened and unknown, the forces of the Solar Logos would imperfectly touch you. Therefore, be awake and in tune through your God Station with all the awakened Logi throughout the Kingdom of Light.

66

THE CONTAINMENT OF GOD INBEING

Remember, to correct ill health, incompleteness and limitation of any type, you must first come within and under the positive attention and recognition of your own God Within. Possessing the hyperintuitional faculty, It will, through the instrumentality of your prayers, align you with specific headwaters of Divine Answer.

You contain the splendor and all the aspects of God. Now, through your willingness and control, let them shine out!

WHENEVER it is your experience to witness the conquest of wrong with right, condition yourselves to be ever humble, true and courageous, that Deity's Light may grace your activities with direction.

When during such efforts for the Light you are battle weary, it is suggested that you follow this procedure in realigning and reconditioning your inward bodies and their outermost sheath.

In your first period of remembrance in the morning, after you have practiced alignment, center your consciousness upon God Inbeing in you and ask:

"Holy and complete Divinity enter Thy vessel in me with empowered wisdom and being. Cause the perfect and sacred flame of Thy Spirit Indwelling to circulate through to the outermost rim of consciousness Divinity's enthronement of strengthening. Let the individuality of Thy Adonaic Pres-

ence be reinvested with God Fires of Deity's ensoulment. Now cause the I Am Indwelling to emanate purely and emphatically the wavelengths of true and invincible individuality based upon and supported by God Inbeing. Engender the frequencies of the Causal World bathing and touching me in such a manner as to quicken my Soul's reception of new and sustained God Life.

"In this region of existence, the powers active around me are alchemical, creative, magical, healing and enlivening."

Recollecting this reality, you will continue your treatment by saying:

"Powers of God currents, enter my Soul or character with fresh strengthening. Endow me in every vestment of this nature with the realized reception of these frequencies from the highest courts and regions of creativity and renewal. Let all which is unfinished, dull and imperfect in my Soul body now receive the grace of Soulic rekindling or quickening of a permanent kind. Let all the hollow areas be filled with Light. May all that is weak be cleansed through the transformation of character strengthening. I welcome into my Soulic consciousness every degree of joyous enlightenment to which I may be worthily attuned.

"Prayerfully I ask that my mental vehicle be purified by the forces of deepened aspiration. I pledge myself to think in an upward direction per-

sistently. Let my outreaching thoughts touch and meet those areas of mental power which, when contacted, bless me through the releasement of their good and God-contained energetic ideas.

"I invite new, true, happy and expansive realizations and certainties of endless and enduring reality. Above all things, in my mind, let me know God-containment.

"Divine Source of my own being, I pray Thee, through the energizing of Thy Spirit Indwelling in me, to enter and bring to peace my desire nature. Teach and aid me toward the building of a more beautiful and trustworthy astral vehicle. I desire the good. I vow to feel and to desire upwardly, likewise. I center my feelings and my desires upon those higher reaches of emotion that will give beauty, substance and transformation to my feeling and desiring faculty.

"Send through into my energies the God Fires of increased and heightened energy and health. I make my promise to act vertically too, wanting always and thinking always of the forces which will bring about health and maintained and improved energy in the outermost vehicles.

"For my physical sheath, Divine God, I ask for cleansing, for regeneration, as well as for the blessed inflow from the central God Fires which shall ever impart an acceleration of all the members which form the united physical body. I live God-

wardly even in the physical envelope residing on earth, for I promise to remember in this most outward form that I am centered in God, that I contain God's vast and powerful life. I will do my utmost to welcome, to permit, and to enable God-containment to become a visible reality in my physical being."

When you learn to do this type of treatment work with practiced skill you will realize increased flow of baptismal power from the Holy Spirit. May you become so centered in Light that darkness cannot exist wherever you, in God-containment, shall live and move and have your being.

THE IMPORTANCE OF CHOICE

Preparation for discipleship begins at any time an individual is consciously ready and prepared to make his happiness—the goal and heartbeat of his existence—the conquest of all that binds him and separates him from Light or God.

To become a disciple the most important decisive quality which an individual must wield is that of *choice*. Up to this point you have had to achieve character and therefore your conscious behavior has been directed toward the subjective. Thus from the time of dedication to completion of discipleship, the signal quality for your attention is choice. Momently you must choose between disciplined effort and relaxed slipping back into the shadowed fancies and enchantments of the glamorous darkness. In your choice to move forward and to be finished with infidelity, procrastination and half-heartedness, you come by degrees that are measured by your longings ever closer to Godly achievements.

INVITE heavenly drafts of empowerments and polarize your bodies in their Light in order that you be not burdened with formulas and techniques for spiritual use.

Find a way to keep your mind free of confusion. Learn to think clearly and to act concretely at every moment you are in possession of yourself. Allow no one to rob you of peace.

Remember, only that rest which contains spiritual repose contains value.

Let the personality fires of extremism die out, and enjoy the incoming and the infusing of your outward life with your Soul's dominion. Through Divinity's means, let the Soul qualities residing in you come forth into fuller expression in your outer life.

EACH OF YOU is enshrined with his own sacred and beautiful purpose. There is a Guardian Spirit related to your life objective and all of its releasements. If you will remember this Guardian of your Soul's sacred purpose you will be helped to be true, to have essential vision, decisive powers, and Masterly conduct in your outward world. Failing this, your objectives falter, your purpose recedes, you become tardy in the fulfillment of what you are commissioned to do. Therefore, do not permit the world to be your temptress. Do not allow a lackadaisical nature to be your jailer. Through the alertness of your listening, keep holy and one-pointed your reverent communion with the Guardians of Spiritual Purposes that they may give you valor and that you may accomplish your God-born duties without resistance from yourself or from the exterior world.

If you would have your whole life encompassed by the guidance of the Lord Christ and His Hierarchy that your inner and outer affairs might then align themselves with Divine Will, this must be your effort:

You must hunger and thirst for righteousness as though you were dying for need of these nutriments. By keeping the consciousness swept clean continuously, by giving attention to the immediacy of Divine Reality, you will become centered. In being centered, poise, wisdom, peace and vivification will be in effect. The self-governed man, perpetually in love with Divinity, draws Divine Presence into the unfoldment of every moment. Center thus upon the prime importance and you will be saved time, you will be well from within, and you will be led of Spirit into ever continuous progress that is both spiritual and practical.

With the days coming, duties mount, but so do the wings of strength with which to lift them. You are intended to welcome into your experience the symbolical wings of spiritual soaring. Realize that these wings are indicative of actual growth. You should have their symbol about you always. Each time you meet a soul testing, keep this thought before you: "Out of this endeavor must come not only increased knowledge and forbearance, but new *wings*." The great Angels have achieved the symbolical display of their Soul victories which are seen by your inspired artists as wings. These are never symbolical of a faculty which aids them in travel, but are simply the arrangement in their auras of powers which are added as the American Indian chiefs won and added their feathers by valor. For every birth of new incentive or decisive consecration, or of surrender to that which is right, you too achieve in your own aura elements which are your "wings"—*new* ones for *new* victories.

LIVING from the Soul level requires the use and giving of general exemplifications of love. The love which is outflowing from the Soul knows genuineness, tenderness, purity, as well as deep interest that amounts nearly to a concern for those loved. This love is wholly without condemnation; it sees imperfection but because of what it sees, more love is outpoured. Yet this love likewise possesses wisdom, knows good judgment, knows when to be outgiving and, because love must be earned by its recipients, when to keep faith while love is reserved. When you live from your Soul level you are mature. There is no childish pride, no excuses, no evasions, no rationalizations. There is only an admittance of truth about oneself. He who lives from the Soul level is reverent at all times and he beholds much that increases his worship. That which he sees of the Soul revealing itself in others but quickens and extends his own reverence. He who lives from the Soul is kind and unselfish. He would bring the entire world into the realization of earned happiness. He who lives from the Soul level possesses self-control. He likewise knows self-command of his mental faculties. There is no absentmindedness about him; for when this trait is present, self-will is very strong. Soul consciousness means self-recollectedness and self-possession without willfulness.

These are seed thoughts for you to use as key-notes for each day and for repeated efforts until your progress in self-conquest wins new footholds in discipleship.

BE ACTIVE in releasing and mastering instinctive inertia and resistance by approaching every such conquest with the thought, for example: *"I will not permit excitement or irritability to be expressed in this moment when I feel their promptings. Rather do I choose to express peace, love and patience before this person and because of this person."*

On another occasion you will say: *"My body prefers rest, but I choose to see that its muscles are made supple, healthy and vigorous through right exercise. My instinctive nature chooses that which is pleasurable to its tastes, but I choose that which edifies and fortifies the inner man through the wise ordering, preparing, and using of wholesome, nourishing foods."*

In the realm of your conduct with your fellow-men, it is always a wise practice to put into being, to manifest through every faculty and vehicle, the loyalty and the beauty of spiritual brotherhood. If your habit of regarding those who are close and cherished as spiritual kin becomes firmly fixed, you will be conditioned and prepared to meet all souls upon this same requisite level. Your spiritual exercises are only dutiful when taken without forethought or creative consideration. Remember the worlds of Light, of power, of beauty and fulfillment that can nurture and transform every action and thought if only you will place your endeavors, however humble and simple they may be into the presence or the foreground of these surrounding realities. Life cannot be methodical, forced or routine in the dutiful manner when Eternity with its long-range importance and creativity is remembered and *invited into* every act.

THOSE who come into that period of life wherein God instruction and Christ service need to occupy their efforts, do not lose their families nor their friends. They simply place them within the watchfulness of the Eternal and, still loving them, move as disciples into a wholly different field of living. The new associations, both physical and superphysical, form links that are greater in spiritual significance than the personal ties one has had to have courage to surrender. When you receive word from your family say to yourself, *"This is my earth family. I love them even as I love my brothers and sisters who work around me—who belong to my eternal family."* You must bring your thoughts and your affections for all up to the par and expressive of the depth you know for your own kin.

Do not forget that when you enter a life of discipleship, instruction and unfoldment are your primary needs and joys. No longer must human dependence and attachments mean as much to you as the fulfillment of your first essential—oneness in an ever deepening sense with the enfolding, eternal God. Look not backward nor familyward, but forward into the present and into the field of the future as well as into Eternity, for this is the realm out of which your deepest joys and your most valuable experiences must come.

It is advisable for individuals who are midway through their physical incarnation, if at all possible, to sever their ties with old things, that they do so by erecting a new home which will contain new facilities and furnishings which are symbolic of the new life powers and blessings and beauties into which they have consciously entered. Such a change may involve human or financial sacrifice. This is a small price to pay for the fullness of benefit to be gained by living in agreement with that which one knows. There is no loss for the disciples who build in utter trust. To them will flow the imperishable gifts of Spirit and their lives will reveal unmistakable signs of Divine Overshadowing.

A tremendous effort must be made to break old habits of fear, self-curtailments, and of false economies. It is not wise to deny oneself the good, the beauty, and the comfort one would give to another. In this season of your unfoldment you must enjoy that which you would wish for others. You must invite and even purchase beauty knowing that not only you shall enjoy the power of this spiritual investment, but others shall likewise reap the benefit by their beholding and sensing the beauty emanations which you have chosen to visibly enshrine your hearthstone.

Look for those real values which are abiding and which you may afford if your choice and your trust are deepened sufficiently to contain them.

These suggestions should be thoughtfully considered by all persons who seek to embody this life of discipleship. Luxury is not to be condoned; but in your exercise of choice, it is well to encourage beauty—beauty and simplicity—with all the mechanical facilities possible, making life as free as can be outwardly fashioned through wise and trustful living. When you come into this field your outward affairs are within the attention of the Christ Hierarchy. When spiritual principles are trusted to the fullest, it will be possible for you to lift the level of your environment.

WE will advance immediately into a further survey of the discipleship your inner selves desire and by which they will benefit during seasons when you consciously aspire toward self-conquest.

Added to the thoughts already shared with you concerning powers and qualities you are to exercise, enlist with them the quality of *discrimination*. Man's most conspicuous lacking need is that of God-love in preference to self-love. When he advances into studies of this nature his most stringent requirement becomes that of discrimination. You will need, through much more thoughtful living, to better evaluate the persons around you, both known and unfamiliar. Before making decisions, you will need to re-evaluate your desires and motivations. When the drafts of temptation blow into your conscious field of attention, you will require controlled reorientation; and this phrase refers to a development which must be worked with in

79

times which are not tried. When the drafts from the lower regions chill you with their sudden pronouncements of testings, your formerly gathered control must be galvanized into preparedness for a new decisiveness and conscious rejection to be pronounced.

Many are possessed of natural discrimination. They are intuitionally aware of those to whom they may speak about these sacred Truths, and those before whom they must be quiet regarding them. If one lacks such inward direction he must say nothing concerning any of the great and sacred Truths or confidences. Let the persons with whom he deals prove themselves, in time and by actions, ready or unready for mutual sharings. A former state of impulsiveness can only be conquered if that impulsiveness is recognized and admitted. Frequently, impulsive gifts accomplish as little as gifts withheld. For that reason, learn to evaluate before you act or speak, considering all sides—your own, your neighbor's, the state of evolution you have achieved, the time in world history. Ask yourself when seized by the draft of impulsiveness, *"Is this wisdom? Has this desire of mine the motivation simply of freeing myself from anguish over the plight of another, or will my action have a long range effect for good upon him? Is he prepared to benefit within, to be wiser, stronger, and more appreciative because of my trust?"*

80

These are the kind of statements you will make to yourselves in cultivating greater discrimination.

So often your love would be kind, and this is right. But the placement of your affection and your giving may be very poorly chosen, and such giving on your part might much more intelligently serve a known and public cause.

Always when tried, strive to recollect, to gather in your moorings through reasoning as to whether the thing or the act your emotions are prompting you to do will stand the light of public acceptance, or whether it will merit the light of approval on your own part a decade hence. You are no longer to be prompted by mere desire, for such desires are repetitious and they lead you only into territories of even greater desires. When desires are harnessed to reason and to long-lasting, spiritual purposefulness, you then will find yourself unashamed of them.

The final point for this reflection is one of *trust*. It is important that you trust persons, causes, time and life itself. What you trust may not always be what you imagine in every detailed case, but you will strike a good average, and in the long run, develop increasing gains over former experiences when dealing with human beings by expressing the quality of trust. Your trust must act as a strong searchlight which will concentrate upon bringing Light and warmth to the inward selves of those upon whom you focus. Trust does not warrant any lack of discrimination, or any lack of self-respect in another's regard. Keep your balance; keep your own proper orientation before all souls. But those to whom you would give the bestowal of trust, you will need to trust spiritually all the way. When you have this kind of regard for those whom your love selects as worthy you should endeavor to be largehearted enough, patient enough, wise enough to overlook the pricks, discomforts, resentments and annoyances of the outer self of your friend. Your interest is not to be focused upon his outer personality. Your searchlight—the large, penetrating and powerful searchlight of spirit—must focus upon and remember only his inner self which you love and which is receiving nourishment, warmth and spiritual quickening through your trust. If he is not what you had imagined, he will be helped to become better if you persist in focusing Light upon him which penetrates to his inner depths.

This would not be a wise course for you to follow with all men at present because there are times when deceivers veil their hypocrisies, and most humans lack the discrimination to detect them. But focus this loving warmth of trust upon those more innocent, truly endeavoring children of life, and witness to what degree man can blossom under such treatment. In time your discrimination will be more greatly perfected and the manner in

which you deal with others can wield a wider arc
of pure inclusiveness.

As DISCIPLESHIP ASPIRANTS, you come under the
watchful attention of members of the Christ Hierarchy who know the value and extent of your efforts. Some of you do not succeed, mentally and
spiritually, in the dedication of your daily efforts.
However, if your conduct is aligned and truly well
directed, you can be sure that a structural foundation is being built which shall lead to the unfoldment of inner experiences of a beneficial kind.

Some of you have days wherein you are spiritually awake. These days pass and you come into a
period which is like tunneling. You are surrounded
by darkness and none of your efforts seemingly
brings you in touch with the Light. These are only
repetitions of your lack of steadfastness in the past.
They must be borne. It is well to remember during
such periods—perhaps of rebellion, temper, irritability and lack of attunement—that though the environment is not one of ease or one which delights
you as do your finer moments, still this period can
be made meaningful. Testings can be extinguished
the more rapidly if you will consecrate yourselves
anew while meeting them. In this regard, the type
of case which offers the most resistance is found in
that temperament which takes things easily and
does not consider fully and deeply enough the im-

portance of such opportunities in the history of one's total advancement.

THERE is a very great need among discipleship candidates for a conquest of *rationalization*. It is suggested that each of you study this very word and come to a fuller understanding of its meaning. Too frequently do you make excuses for that which you do. You must instead learn to face reality and to admit mistakes. Admit what has been done through poor judgment, forgetfulness, or neglect; and in your acknowledgment of a mistake you are then able to go beyond it. Through your humble acknowledgment will come open realizations of the thresholds of powers and abilities which lie beyond that weakness for the conquest of the weakness. Remember this discipline: Let there be no more rationalizing excuses for doing what you have done. Instead, freely admit what you have done. Express your regret, include your self-forgiveness and then *will* that in the future it shall no longer exist.

WHEN the heart is ready, Light enters it. Often the progress of discipleship trainees is watched by Elder Brothers and Sisters of the Christ Hierarchy with pleasure. Some discipleship candidates who possess more difficulties to conquer seem to progress more slowly. Others who are less encumbered are more readily receptive. Nevertheless it needs always to be remembered, whether the pupil has much or little to master, that it is the intention and the will of the pupil which matters, and this is studied with impartial interest. A snail's pace of growth has the same value for the one who is encumbered, as an advancement of a far greater distance for the one more swift.

Has it been asked of you, as the apostle Paul asked those whom he met, "Have ye received the Holy Spirit since ye have believed?" All disciples at some time perceive that they either maintain the activation of the Holy Spirit as a result of their studies, or they see how empty and far from this reality they are. Because you are in conscious alignment with resources of truth that are steadfast and extremely influential, you (and all like you with conscious knowledge) share the need to practice the arts of spirituality. You should be *naturally* loving, naturally thoughtful, patient, refined and self-governed. The sign of your identification with the Hierarchy must be one of recognized consecration.

In no way does this mean to be pious in an assumed manner, nor should your demeanor be one of struggle to be what you are not! Thinking of the Brotherhood and Sisterhood of Unfolded Souls, and perceiving in Them the recognition of God's own promise of perfection should make the futur-

85

ity of your budding powers more evident and realized. Being attuned to the Hierarchy by your conscious dedication has its own refining, beautifying and purifying effect. You cannot act grossly, curtly or meanly when you remember the Lord Christ and His Host of Servers. Recollecting the reality of Their living presence brings simultaneous communing with the Source of God Life. Whenever you think of them you will also have quick flashes of insight, more intuitional than intellectual, of the states of consciousness and the equipment of powers beyond Masterhood.

We charge you to be a nobler, more honest, more unselfish and more helpful person now and henceforth. Let the nobility of spiritual remembrance reach out to the outermost circle of your life—in the letters you write, the car you drive, the manner in which you keep your home, the mood with which you prepare food, and the attitudes with which you regard others. Being one with life that is momently becoming more conscious of completeness, you must verify faith, consecration, deepest love, and high courage. In the days which are at hand you will of necessity be required to choose between the way of the Holy Spirit and the self-centered way. *Which do you choose now?*

Allow the witness of all the powers which accompany the great Brotherhood and all who are within it to reach you in every part. Dwell thoughtfully within a deeper awareness of the realm of Eternity which is your homeland. Consciously receive, accept and yearn for inhalations of pure refreshment —for those drafts of Spirit which invigorate the mind, cleanse the emotions, and empower the physical instrument whenever you recollect them.

LIFE'S MOVEMENTS continue in cyclic and measured order. How many steps have you taken, consciously measured? Behold the wonder, grandeur, the ecstasy of life as it moves about us! The hours have their charged patterns as the sun's movement reveals new areas emphasized by light and others harmonized by shadow. So you must learn to enjoy intense sunlight when it is upon you. The sunlight of inner currents from Eternal Shores intensifies the regions in you which are ready for Light. There are days when your mind is under a shadow. It is restive, troubled and confused. But on such occasions there is an area within you receiving the sunlight of Spirit. Perhaps it would be felt as well-being in the physical form, or emotional exaltation of a constructive kind.

Again your circumstances might bring the sight of the Soul to your mental recognition. Learn to see yourself as you are—partly in the sunlight of spiritual response and partly in the shade. Be unashamed of the shadows while you are endeavoring to make the mind, or some member of your

87

nature, worthy to receive at all times the blessing of the sunlight of Spirit.

Do NOT FEEL that there is anything too difficult for you to conquer. Focus your attention upon the changing and lifting of your mood, your appetite, your habit. See it in all its clarity of exposed weakness. Upon it apply the cleansing antiseptic of resolute uprooting. As soon as you determine to take your most glaring weakness in hand, before the sanctuary of your Spirit's inmost presence, you shall be enabled to gain moment by moment release from the tentacles of instinctive oppressions. Say to yourself, *"There is nothing I cannot do when the Spirit within me is allowed to give Its help. I can do anything through aligned, centered and attentive consciousness of the Supreme Spirit that lives through me."*

Therefore, strive to eliminate your vagrancies of thought, your impurities of mood, and your physical obsessions by consciously opening the door of the Spirit's will and penetration and forgiveness upon them.

May your mornings, afternoons and evenings of life be well spent. Then indeed, whether there is outer sunshine or clouds in the sky, your consciousness will be illumined and filled with the perpetual Light of your Spirit's day.

88

ATTITUDES OF DISCIPLESHIP

*When man learns of the most prized gift in
all of life to be achieved, every other objective should pale by contrast to his longing
for the obtainment of this requisite gift—
awareness of Deity in and through one here
and now.*

Your difficulties in regard to maintaining spiritual communion grow out of your imperfect
realization of discipleship. This achievement needs
to be always in the foreground of your consciousness. Your state of mind, your habits, and your
very efforts should be regulated, controlled and
purified by this development. You expect, and quite
naturally, flares of inspiration and new heights attained in momentous realizations. These goals are
achievable only when discipleship is a practiced
reality. Your concentration needs to emphasize
discipleship in preference to the upsurges of spiritual recognitions.

Realize that discipleship begins your residence
in the higher altitudes of consciousness while you
yet wear human bodies. Discipleship, because of its
active state of awareness, is of much greater consequence than the transient, comforting pleasures of

self-indulgent living. Therefore, give yourself to an untiring use of discipleship's disciplines.

FOR several lifetimes a devotee, or a pupil-to-be, unfolds through that stage called *probation*. At this stage God-worship should be constant, particularly as the expression of innermost longing for Divine Reality. The application of spiritual principles to the growth of character requires vigilant study by those who are aspiring on this general level of development. When the desire for God is equalled by a willingness to change and to grow spiritually, the individual is slowly and watchfully graduated into the state of *discipleship*.

With discipleship comes a voluntary surrender of the entire self to the work or the service of God. Henceforth the attitude of the disciple includes this over-all service, this life pledge wherever and in whatsoever he is outwardly doing.

Secondly: Perceiving and executing the continuous desire for more realization of God, a disciple gives himself naturally and faithfully to consistent daily growth. His path is the path to self-mastery. His tools are the hours and the circumstances within the hours with which he works to create for himself the goal of attainment—Mastership. Discipleship possesses the need for patience, for exactness of application, as well as for flexibility of consciousness which faces God.

90

Thirdly: The Divine Work related to earth is unfinished. Every Perfected Son and Daughter of God becomes an artisan invested with a deliberate knowledge of the Great Plan. Each disciple, loving God, lends himself to the completing of the Plan. In his mind and within the territory of his life, the people around him and the edifices of his outward world become a part of his responsibility. For that reason, the disciple's yearning for the improvement and the unfoldment of persons, works, and lives of young creation, moves within his circle of obligation. The disciple grows by his extended and deepened worship of the Divine, by his freeing others like himself, by aiding younger lives such as the creatures, and by lending his support to unfinished works.

The center of a disciple's deepest testing lies within the jurisdiction of his own free will. A disciple could easily become perfected without many hindrances were he responsible only for deepened God-love and true self-giving helpfulness to others. The truth of the matter is, however, that beside these two supreme requirements, the field of his own free will determines the rate of his progress and the measure of his fulfillments. A disciple's free will *can* be made to serve creatively and one-pointedly the Eternal Plan. The stronger and finer the discipleship consciousness, the more ingenious will be his application of imagination, thoughtful planning, and perpetually renewed dedication. It is within this area that the disciple's true inner state of advancement most vividly appears. Being under no compulsion, persuasion or demand to do good, to embrace new spiritual customs, the disciple may easily, in these hours or periods, retreat into self-centeredness and inaction. Given incentives from his two supreme objectives, and being of the character Mastership invites, a worthy disciple will, in these hours freed from routine or guided objectives, live so creatively, so attuned and at-one with the all-inclusive God Plan, that for him there are no off-moments, periods of dejection or times of confusion. For him there is activity self-determined, of the order which leads to peace and to achievement regardless of the fields through which the disciple needs to travel—financial, material, social, educational or cultural.

Go into your fields of daily occupation with the will and the heart devoted to God. See in the preparation of food or the directing of young minds, your creative opportunity to improve and extend your own discipleship and to radiate its qualities unself-consciously as energies of enlivenment into the lives you bless. Assume your duties as obligations to the Divine. Put into your endeavor, by way of the state of consciousness, that integrity, that worshipful love which will keep you open to Divine Presence persistently.

Let every morning of your life find God newly revealed!

THE great and flaming need is to learn to love, to worship, to give oneself to God before all else— before even the pleasure of one's own commitments. For this reason, that which stands in the way of genuine and wholehearted humility for all channels is usually the focus unknowingly of interest in themselves, their lives, and their approaches. These have to be swept out. Discipleship can come much more readily when an individual learns just that simple point—to be in love with God more than centered within himself or outwardly engrossed in the activities and loves of others.

Discover new ways to achieve this outgoing surrender and giving of the self to the worship of the whole at every moment. God is here. When attuned to this Presence the objective personality will relax, the mind will be righted, the character placed in direct alignment, strength will come and the authority of Spirit will speak through one who is forever in love with God.

So often, because you are human, you think you must actually see before you that which is important and to which you must give obedience. It is more essential to learn that the greatest truth, the most important powers and infinities are invisible; and their invisibility forms the goal by which new

93

states of consciousness are conquered. Awareness eclipses sight. Therefore, at every moment that which is invisible to you must be observed *by your conscious endeavor to remember it*. This practice of remembrance should include not only Infinite God but also God individualized in Perfected Souls. Then the ardor of your humility begins by recollecting these essentials at every moment, and by living in such a way that honor, blessing and service are given to these importances.

Even as physical light shines in your world, so now do the Light of the spiritual sun and its loftier radiations touch you and purify you atomically in the beinghood of your own vehicles of Spirit.

Do not permit obstacles to obstruct your consciousness. Chase the shadows and be impervious to the pressures through your own accessibilities to God-Light.

KNOW that your days are abundantly filled, both with duties and joys, because you have come to the plane of development where you must function as an outpost of the Christ Hierarchy. Neither dread nor fear the overload of responsibilities, but hasten your steps in growth and increase your prayers for wisdom in the application of these duties.

RECOLLECT at all times that God is your benefactor and His influence flows through your life. No

other person, power or event must be permitted to
supercede your recognition of this surrounding
spirit of goodness—or God. Your personal work is
to allow your acquaintanceship and adventure into
contact and companionship with this spiritual benefactor to occupy your time, thoughts and major
efforts. Secondly, learn detachment from personal
estimations and considerations, and approach all
things with universal and impersonal interest and
helpfulness.

IT IS URGENT that you realize the significance of
preparedness. When life surprises you, even catch-
ing you off guard with unexpected events of great
spiritual consequence, who of you would not look
back to ten or twenty years before and realize
anew the amazing unpredictableness of life's progressive, forward movement? Therefore, expect
the unusual, the everlasting joyous, and be pliable,
eager and thankful that you have a physical body
on this earth in which to prove your dedication
and your gifts of Spirit.

As DISCIPLES keep your consciousness centered in
Light and you will know that your future *is* certain
to be one of peace and progress. At one with Light,
your joy, inspiration and education will come from
adventuring into the inner side of your mind and
Soul.

95

Were persons more consciously aware of realities of the higher spheres which they touch with their thoughts they would be continuously entertained, instructed and taught. True association with the Divine more than equalizes the exterior frustrations and imbalances. Become so acquainted with the Light that what your child does, or your neighbor or parent says, is of no personal consequence to you who are centered in understanding and goodwill. Your right attitude will purify and correct the improper attitudes which might be presented to you as tests.

On the physical plane, everyone until Masterhood indulges in some habit which is detrimental to his physical well-being. It might be in the matter of food that you need retraining, simplification and conquest. Or it could be that you do not exercise sufficiently, therefore the drafts within your metabolism are working ineffectually. Or you might be starved for newness, for more recreation as well as for exploration of new physical interests. For that reason seek out and center upon the physical habit which chiefly binds you to weakness, to this imperfect behavior which impairs your expression of lengthened life.

For the rest of your life you should consider that never again will you possess freedom to indulge that vice. Catering to any weakness becomes a conscious vice. It is not for superficial reasons that you are urged to make these releasements. It is because at this stage of unfoldment your necessity to accomplish these overcomings is over-ripe. Cultivate an opposing, constructive value on the physical plane that you have long neglected or never developed. For instance, if you have not had sufficient exercise, then devote yourself to more walking and to doing that which gives your body a little more exertion each day. For those who have not been doing new things or developing new talents, socially or artistically, these inherent potentialities must be introduced to your world. The stimulating and innovative improvements you make will energize and stir others.

In a similar manner, following this plan for the releasement of destructive habits and the installation of their positive counterparts, continue the task of your emotional conquest. In every person prior to Mastership there is much in the astral body requiring healing, purification, harmonizing and refining—all that makes you fearful, causes you to be troubled with anxiety, fills you with impatience, or allows you to give way to irritability. The negative currents which come during these episodes of indulging your weaknesses on the emotional level are sent toward you as well as throughout the planet by obsessive powers. You know by now that they are destructive.

97

See to it that your three lowest centers, the first three chakras, are maintained in quietness and with control during times of unrest and tumult in the world. If your particular weakness tends you toward great excitement, to dramatization of your fears, to self-pity, to attachment, or to any of these weaknesses of the emotional level, see to it that all these things know the light of your daily scrutiny and your unending effort to be freed from them. The nervous temperament particularly requires the opposite constructive values of poise, self-control, detachment, and centered peace.

Those who are phlegmatic in their nature especially need stirring, sensing, feeling, loving, expressing, doing and giving.

On the mental plane your greatest danger lies in your allowing yourself to live mentally within clouds of apprehension, as well as dislikes and all the unholy elements of a diseased consciousness. Next to your Soul body, your mind will possess the best means for your being channeled by your own spiritual resources of protection during years of crisis. To coin a phrase, "Keep your head and your body will be safe." Many times persons erroneously believe themselves safe to dwell perpetually in the shadows of brooding thoughts, of unhappiness, of world fears, or dread of the future. Such reflections are not in order. You must tread that path which leads to the Light and to a channeling of

that Light; and to the dispersing of cesspool-like ac-
cumulations of destructive mental elements. Determine to yourself what your particular negative
mental habit might be, whether it is one primarily
of fear of the unknown, or skepticism, or possibly
the lack of good thorough reasoning. Root out these
imposters from the kingdom of your selfhood—
only you possess the power to dethrone them. However untrained your mind, however untried it
might have been in the past, to encourage good
thoughts of peace, blessing and goodwill, let it now
be secured in the fortress of your spiritual support.

If you allow your mind to be a jungle where all
instinctive things dwell, you can imagine how re-
pulsive would be your consciousness centered in
this tangled growth of impressions released from
the instinctive nature. However, your mind can
become like a garden, it can have the strength and
altitude of a tall mountain peak, or it can have the
wide range of serenity that the sky knows at sunset
on a clear day. In your thoughts, determine to
dwell with the peaks and among the birds and
winged messengers of the skies rather than with
the creeping things that belong to the subhuman
level. You are asked to accept this not as a discipline, but rather as a program for bringing yourself up to the level of receptivity of this strongest
and finest order.

You are urged to bring yourself to the best order

you can achieve. Commune with your Soul Self and cultivate a constructive attitude from that level. Out of the diversity of many gifts, choose one whose acquaintance you will endeavor to encourage, be it intuition, or the flow of inspirational powers expressed in painting, in singing, or in writing. Or cultivate the channelship of the healer, or the consciousness of positive receptivity to Divine instructions daily. Whatever you choose, be faithful to your training of this creative choice during all of the opportune days before you.

It is well to do your utmost to bring yourself to balance and to make the foundation of your three lower bodies strong enough to support the wonderful edifice of spiritual service that will come with complete preparedness. You are being urged to move only in that direction where you should already be traveling.

PRIDE is the result of the self being centered where God is absent. To conquer pride, God Presence must be embodied, welcomed, watched, enjoyed and received in every pore, with every longing, with every breath until man comes to that place where he knows that what he was *first* was made by God, the Creator. What he is becoming is the work of the Creator too, for without God's power impinging upon man, how would he know how to grow? There is no place for pride because all that man is, he has become through God. There is a place for self-respect which encourages good conduct so that one does not step lower, but keeps himself on a plane on which he has determined to function. In every other respect, the self must be taught to step aside and be filled with Divine power so God can bring out the hidden individuality in each one.

REGARDING rigidity, watch what you do not like because the manner by which you profess your displeasure, your disapproval, or your criticism reveals either rigidity or that wisdom which is adaptive and creative. Have prejudices no longer. See the good in everything, even to the gnats and the venomous snakes whose existence prompts man to develop that kind of consciousness that is impervious to annoyances and free from carelessness.

Focus at all times upon Infinite Light, for you can only progress by the Light of Individuality rising within you to meet the Life and Light of God the whole.

THE NEED for childlikeness is the key to pride's conquest. To all those who have been proud, childlikeness will soften, relax, purify, and eliminate that pride from which they have suffered and which has cast about them crusts or shells of hardness. These encrustations have shut out Light; and

101

their beings are starved for that which comes from true, full and deep breathing of all of God.

Therefore, learn to have the heart of a child in its joyousness, in its trust, its all inclusive love. If one can achieve this as a permanent quality, one's health and whole being will benefit. The child is not responsible for making judgments or for creating standards. The child accepts the edicts and the laws of Spirit from those who are spiritually older and wiser. It is therefore difficult for the proud soul to completely surrender himself to another's way.

LEARN to think of the other person before you do of yourself. Most persons who live alone are inclined toward extreme self-interest which eclipses the interests and needs and wishes of other persons. Said simply, learn to be unselfish, to be strongly God-centered, and to be dependable at all times and in all places.

The need in one life to change from positiveness to a selfless, humble personality is so important a change that there are few who ever make it in one incarnation. For the overcoming of self-centeredness it is needful for each of you to see this accomplishment of the completely selfless individuality as the highest attainment of your life; for you, spiritual enlightenment is not nearly as important as the alteration of your personality from lower to

102

higher. When that is gained, or even attempted, there will come intimations of clearance and at-one-ment with the Eternal which promise the maintained enlightenment. Think less, you who need it, upon illumination, and more upon the achieving of this transition and transference of the self-emphasis so that it can be placed where emphasis rightly belongs—on the pure, on the completely, positively humble, spiritual self.

RECALL frequently every day that behind the screen of the invisible are Those who love you and who are your friends, beyond any friendship you understand on earth. Your strength, your happiness, your growth can be quickened by a recollection of this reality.

ALL LIFE has the ability of being fresh and engrossing. It is the person that makes his own events exquisite or very commonplace. Approach the various exercises shared with you with new intent and with the feel of need. Should they become stale, it means that the individual is becoming stale, not the processes, not the realities, not the powers of invigoration. Therefore, the disciple must ventilate his own aura, his own thoughts, his own motivations, and his own needs until in that clearer ventilation there is no more staleness—only beauty of God entrance. Then begin again the given techniques and each one will be seen as a gleaming jewel, priceless and of infinite worth.

IN THE COURSE of one's life it is not uncommon to be confronted with routine work which is not important for the advancement of the disciple's inward self. If this be your circumstance, remember it is then yours to do for discipline and for the bringing forth of more willing service. In other words, in previous lives those who have this kind of duty to perform have been rebellious at routine labor. Now, before they can advance, they have routine service to meet and to do highly, without complaint and without compromise but with wholehearted, spiritual, radiant endeavor instead. In place of thinking upon weariness, upon the difficulties of meeting material minds and the pressures of commercial service, *meditate on being a spokesman for the Eternal at the point from which you serve.* When you so concentrate and serve, the Eternal will feed you with its energies and supply you with its idealism. You will return to your home rested and you will have more than enough to recollect at night about the good things that were made possible through your standing in that place, a server between Eternity and the three-dimensional prison of physical life.

YOUR SOUL must be bathed in the flame of holy

eagerness. It must know that these miracles of communion with Divine frequencies are everywhere present, and that one can touch such a livewire of contact if he but achieve within himself the surrendered dedication of all his being to such Light. In general, this problem is typical of all those who take for granted the gifts of God and who live too much in the manner of just trying to accept rather than to seek with eager desire the more that is beyond the horizon.

Another point: Increase your worship of the unknown, of the mysteriously ever-present reality of the wonder which is about you. Focus within the foreground of the attention, whenever you close your eyes at prayer, all your treasured memories of highlighted teachings which bring you face to face with this transcendent possibility, and let that reminder be your primer to energize your mood for discovering more of God.

To INQUIRE how one can develop greater faith is to present one of the supreme queries, for faith is related to everything man needs, all which he desires, and all which he must live in order to become enlightened. It is at the same time very simple, yet difficult to achieve. The simplicity referred to is observed in the man who is devoted to God. His whole heart is opened toward the sunlight of God and he is aware of this Light. But when he goes within himself, within the cloister of his own mundane interests, he no longer stands in that precious Light. The warmth, the wholesomeness, the happiness of it no longer nurture him from within. You are urged, therefore, to stay in the Light. You have only to remember God and that you need God more than breath; that you must love God more than self or any other person or pleasure.

If you could practice this unbrokenly even for a day, illumination could take place at any moment. The trouble is, man in general is as yet too fickle and too self-bound. Lessons of this nature are given you to help loosen your earth-bound conditions. Remember, the shores of infinity touch you. Let their waves bring into your receptivity the gifts and strengthenings that come from deepened faith.

FAITH IS A VIGOR of the Soul that summarizes all the elements of conquest and idealizes all the possibilities which must be achieved, and then bombards, penetrates and ensouls whatever is needing the effects of its energies. There are levels of faith and each one of them contains trust; but in the highest planes of this causative power you will discover positive command. You will find an intuitional giving of Causal force itself, stamping upon the imperfect the pattern of the perfect.

YOUR PROBLEMS most often come through your periods of stubbornness—of being out of tune in

106

your outflowing periods. Do not personify so emphatically these outflowing tides you experience. Do not turn them to personal exaggerations. With greater reverence, with the realization that your childhood, and manhood or womanhood which is coming to flowering within you is capable of transcending these immaturities, you will come to the patience God feels toward you and you will have greater patience for yourself. But in all things, be steadfast in your awareness that your treasure lies not in the world, not in love, not in the home, not in success, nor even in your own growth. *Your treasure lies in your being self-emptied and God-filled;* and in that God-filling is the treasure of the discovery of what keeps and makes and maintains life in gracious beauty.

To you, a day of freedom and emancipation from your former considerations of yourself—a day filled with new receptions of life as it can be and is intended to be realized here.

WHEN MAN first receives the outpouring of communion with higher dimensions, his response is good. When the initial eagerness passes, however, he must learn to recognize the arid desert regions between the oases of inner receptivity. It is his conduct and the level of his consciousness during the arid periods which determine the frequency of his further contacts with the Infinite.

Your desert seasons invite much improvement. Into them should flow more idealization, more picturization, true, constant use of the exercises you have found valid—especially those which are useful to your own temperament. Keep your character growth at par with the speed of your heart's longings and with the rate of your physical employments. Bring down into objective consciousness the ecstasy of knowing and sensing and believing in the Christ.

You cannot salute the Lord Christ and be open to the spheres of endless life which He represents and still indulge in sadness and confusion. Take upon yourself such duties as do not hide or diminish the Light. Yet in all things, even in the spiritual realities, there is need for manifestation and for work timed by inner awareness. The more work you can undertake in attunement, the stronger shall be your recognized growth in control. Merely to commune with God without steadfast action on the outer plane of life keeps you a tenant on the roof rather than a user of all the floors and rooms of your beinghood. Bring through into the ground floor, therefore, some of the beauty that you have glimpsed upon the rooftop during your higher attunements.

THERE are three states of consciousness in which you must learn to work effectively before your in-

108

ward endeavors are knowingly fruitful. The first is called the *cohesive* or corporate state of mind. The second is the *reflective* state while the third is the *subjective*.

The use of the term *cohesive state of consciousness* is meant to include all types of reasoning in which analysis, good judgment, the application of noble thoughts, their deduction and estimation are utilized. The cohesive state covers that territory which ranges between your very objective world and the world of your highest practical thoughts. Even Divinity itself becomes practical when you consider it analytically and examine it in such a way as first to distinguish and then later utilize its properties.

What you have received thus far shall serve as seed elements from the highest octaves of spiritual growth. These seed forms travel from the subjective realm within you gradually into the very cohesive or practical realm of your mind. Thus it will always be.

You shall henceforth deal in your objectivity, both in reasoning and in action, with that spiritual matter which has in this way reached your most concrete level. Those forms which now are in your subjective state of interest may be manifest in your practical utilization a week hence, or within a year, or even a decade. It is needful that you know more about these states since in time you must be occupied on all three planes in a very conscious manner. Cohesive meditation therefore, at some part of your conscious remembrance intervals, will summarize what you have learned in relation to Mastership in terms like these:

"Mastership is a condition which begins with continuous unfoldment. I am striving for Mastership. It applies to this day and to my application now of the remembrances, energies and archetypes that will still me and activate me at the same time, spiritually and objectively. In regard to what I need for self-conquest, all the powers of its elements reside around me in quietness. They are there as a background and move toward and into me at my conscious invitation. Actively in outward endeavor I shall busy myself now, employing my ideal for Mastership, making it real all this day. The detrimental forces about which I have become conscious in myself shall be continuously released and expelled from my conscious being. I summon with every breath and with my life's great need those forces that will keep me attuned to the inflow of my Mastership."

There are many ways in which this is broken up and made more minute. For instance, a person whose mind flits hither and yon is torn with infidelities, with the many attractive enticements from the world, with the distractions of human relationships, and by forces within his own instinc-

110

tive self. Such a person will meditate upon this day, objectively, quietly, with self-containment, concentrating upon the unfoldment of fidelity, upon oneness, and upon the complete coordination of himself and all his tendencies so that all which he includes will be mantled by his genuine dedication to the real.

Therefore, throughout the day cohesive meditative work will be utilized as the remnants from the old nature are seen and are taken up like weeds and brought into the center of one's contact with the real where the Light is strongest. There, in serene surrender to the Supreme, even the remembrance of a weed-like quality is forgotten in the total rapt adoration of the All.

You must learn in your outward consciousness to detect the slightest subtle degree of response to those outward attractions and forces which suggest the old detriments. Instantly, at the slightest indication of these outworn things, you are to remind yourself through cohesive work in consciousness that your entire beinghood, including all your faculties, the circumference of your aura, the extent of your interest, are devoted to oneness, to complete attuned consecration to your Mastership.

Always the subject of Mastership must not be a final end in itself, for this would make you an egotist as boastful as the fabled Lucifer. But you need Mastership and your requirement will always be in the present until that state itself is gained. Your necessity for Masterhood is for that condition of beinghood which can stand the further pressures which come with the onward march of your progress. You want Mastery's wholeness and peace, and its ability to be in command of oneself and of those forces that are outward antagonists. You want the peace of Masterhood in order that the total knowledge which is contained by the Spirit of the Cosmos will be gradually unfolded to your mastered interest.

Thus, once more, you are reminded to be masterly in little things. Overcome subtleties, deceits and falsities. Be true straight through to the center of yourself—with everyone in all situations. Such action may cause displeasure to many—and perhaps some sorrow—but irregardless, you must achieve sincerity and complete integrity. No one else's desires for you must deter your expression of wholehearted affiliation with your own reality. In time your sincere efforts will not hurt. They will bring confidence and strength to those who watch the chrysalis of your unfolding.

Therefore in your remembrance times, think well and deeply regarding Masterhood as it applies at your stage of unfoldment. Concentration, meditation and contemplation on Mastery will prompt your highest level of comprehension and give to your world your deepest measure of service.

112

Reflective meditation includes rational thinking combined with Causal consciousness. This means it is a combination of the best and highest reasoning you possess blended with the activities of those intuitional fires which feed that reasoning. Reflective thought includes states of being which are beyond you, as well as realities of higher dimensions that are not discernible until you have mastered the way to higher thresholds in actual at-one-ment.

Cohesive meditation is occupied by your utilization of those elements of reality of which you know —to which you have thus far awakened. Reflective meditation touches upon all that which you have heard on the inner planes at night, as well as in your outward consciousness. Many of these elements you have not considered. They lie idly in your mentality. You are even enabled in reflective meditation to move into spheres of comprehension never experienced heretofore. Moreover, in this state you are given the futurity vision and explanation of powers by which it is possible to judge how and when these needed and more advanced means, exercises and developments may come. Therefore, rejoice in all those methods which improve your facility for doing reflective work properly. It uses the highest aspects of your mentality as well as the whole of your Soul or Causal body. It enables you to enter these higher realms, to dwell in them temporarily in your outward existence, and by prac-

113

tice you can learn to return quickly and easily to higher realms where power is expressed in magnitude beyond your finite conception.

The *subjective* state of consciousness is wholly one that utilizes the Soul body and the will of the Adonai within. It executes all that it conceives. It draws the patterns of what must come. Reflective meditation does that too, although it is through your own channelship, highest reasoning and idealism that subjective impressions are given. They are impressed upon your mental faculty, after which they are directed into your own orbit. Very few reach this state with any sense of constancy. In your highest moments—a few occasions in a lifetime—you come to it, usually by way of sorrow or by way of spiritual rapture which often follows some kind of renunciation.

Gates formerly closed to you now open and through these openings it is possible for you to be in touch with what might be termed the super-consciousness. It is also known as the creative, primal, formulative, and electric world of God-energy. The means for reaching this state need emphasis: There must be complete sincerity, no dramatization of self or even of one's rapture in devotion, but a complete, clean, free, natural, sincere yearning to reach out to God, to be in that state where one is surrounded by conscious realization of God's Infinity. Thus, when an individual is most

114

true, and completely, sincerely focused, the intervening states are transcended in a moment and his own Soul contains the cognition and his thoughts are spacious and clothed with the Light in which he finds himself. Again there is no dramatization— only wonder, joy and oneness with the power that is feeding, instructing and infusing one. A man feels as though he were possessed of a thousand eyes, each one reflecting that Light which is about him.

Whenever you are able to achieve subjective meditation you are like a swimmer carried into waters by waves of power beyond your normal ability. True, these high waters and tremendous waves would not be safe to brave persistently. Since God Himself is your security, you can weather the strong currents and the breathtaking beauty of these magnitudes provided that you think clearly while maintaining your grounded contact with the world by aligned living.

Follow your regular beats of attunement with sincere anticipation. In each one, alternate from the practice of cohesive to that of the reflective type of consciousness. Try, but do not be too concerned if you are unable to enjoy subjective meditation. For most novitiates it will seem as though you are only suspended in space, and the space is awesome. Let go of this dread of being overcome by the greatness and vastness of the momentous

115

spiritual power which confronts you. You will become accustomed gradually to it. Return another day for another practice of subjective self-releasement into the ocean of God-inclusiveness. The time will come when this state, which is the result of your thinking and realizations being perceived through the Adonaic Being, will be as natural to you as now in your best moments your Soul experience is realized.

MASTERSHIP begins with the conquest of your highest consciousness and where subjective powers become your particularized strength. The subjective consciousness exists above the mind. It contains both Soulic and Adonaic ranges of energies. In it are life essence, spiritual will, and the whole gamut of Divine powers for your consequent work. It is essential to understand the three states of consciousness described previously, for you shall function in each of them. Relate the analysis and description of these states to your own inner needs. You who come to spiritual thresholds have been strangers to the subjective, or highest spiritual consciousness because of interferences and resistances which arise from your shadow natures. As all the sages of antiquity have disclosed, man contains both a demon and an Angel in his sevenfold nature. The unregenerate shadow nature which influences the lower emotions and the whole territory of the instinctive nature is man's chief enemy until overcome. *The blackest powers in the cosmos do not contain the strength to influence a single one of you that your own indwelling shadow possesses.* You are now being brought into a greater understanding of what you have to accomplish, not only to climb knowingly toward inner freedom in this earthly pilgrimage, but also to attain liberation from the tyrant within. All subversive interests, attractions, fancies, glamours, tests and temptations originate in the shadow nature which needs to be brought under control. Generally speaking, the difference between the Master and the less evolved man is the difference between conflicts and interferences conquered, and those which are still unconquered.

In meditations each day, during some portion of your time's allotment, reflect upon the reality that you shall someday dwell wholly in the subjective region of consciousness which lies above and beyond the mental faculty. For that purpose you should regularly endeavor to climb aspiringly and worshipfully as high as your range of consciousness will enable you to travel. The higher the rise of your consciousness, the greater and wider is your ability to resist and reject the interference of the shadow nature.

There is in everyone a fault similar to faults within the earth that create earthquakes. This might be due to self-indulgence in relation to appetite, sensuality, extravagance, or the permitting of willfulness and self-centeredness of a rampant emotional nature. Whatever your fault might be, therein lies an open door for the shadow nature to rule and to have dominion over you. This satanic influence will even encourage your thoughts and desires toward Mastership in the hope of making you more willful, more independent, and more unknowingly selfish. In fact, tyrannical forces work for independence—to make their own rules with the result that they resist all subjection, surrender, and the giving of obedience to the Light. For this reason, if you yearn for Mastership, there must be at the same time an ever greater self-surrender, an ever more marked love consciousness; for only in that way can Mastership be earned—by sharing.

Think on these things and come to a fuller understanding of what your dangers consist. Realize that wherever you travel, either into new states of consciousness or into halls containing new people, your fault remains with you until it is brought to control and later to conquest. Whatever your fault may be, in time it will become your *primal strength*—the basis upon which all the other God-qualities flow to you with swifter wings.

What you may have done in endeavors toward Light is to allow interferences to depress and to deter you. Let us imagine a person whose fault lies

118

chiefly in the physical region of appetite. He will learn, as he consciously surrenders himself to his task of overcoming, to make a new relationship with food itself. He must build into his desire nature the wholesome and radiant qualities of health. He may, until he is strong, sense the pleasureable attractions of all types of food which once began their influence of death in him. He should be able to move about amidst attractive food temptations; to look upon them with eyes of wisdom, knowing that they are death-dealing. In the same way he needs to make friends with that which will prolong and enhance and beautify his relationship to this physical world through health.

Those in whom the fires of sensuality persist must build up a new relationship to persons. Each sex should look upon the other from the threshold of sisterhood and brotherhood; and in their treatment periods they might say, *"With the exception of the one I have chosen or the one I seek, for whom I save myself, I look upon all women or all men as my sisters and brothers."* If you persist in this regard with enough enthusiasm and interest, you will find in such relationships adventures which are more engrossing than any you previously realized in the old reign when infatuations were permitted with all their enslavements.

For those in whom the darkness of pride persists, in whom self-centeredness continues to block spir-

119

itual progress, a true, genuine and self-surrendered humility toward their need for wholeness requires developing.

You do not have now, and never shall have reason for pride. Therefore be frequently purified by relating yourself to God present within which Itself is wholly, purely, splendidly humble in worship of the Real. You will stand often in the midst of crowds experiencing again the slight tendrils of interference from the shadow nature, but as mastership endeavors continue, you will not allow an uprising of the darkness of pride to hinder you. When conscious of this chief detriment say, "*I reject all evil from my Father's house. My house of being is the house of God. I choose that peace abide herein. May its power be holy and its influence lasting.*"

Rather than to exult in the ashes of empty pride, count it greater gain to move with detachment and with self-surender among many who might otherwise strive to give you praise and adulation.

The purpose of this instruction is to help you reject the shadow nature and develop the dominion of God Presence Within.

Strive to become acquainted with those heights within which are still veiled, knowing that these veils will be removed. Stir your realizations of the heights into a quickened life as you aspire toward the loftiest that you can understand.

After you have used your alignment technique and other preparatory work which the Soul within you chooses to exercise upon a certain day, you will at a pivotal point in your meditation say, *"God is in me; and I am in God,"* recalling and sensing that the Adonai is thus linked with the God Flame. Then continue by saying, *"God is; and I am of God. My Soul encompasses the Light. My mind perceives the real. My emotions aspire toward the good. My energies radiate Light. My physical form embodies and utilizes Light."*

Then using spiritual will idealize and endeavor to say with full consecration, *"I resolve, I aspire, I discriminate, I worship, I glorify God. I am in God, whole complete, centered, and at peace."*

ATTUNEMENT DISCIPLINES

There is no bread like that of Spiritual Truth
to feed man's inner hunger.

IF you want to graduate from the neophyte to the
disciple, it will be necessary for you to give your
best and highest efforts to the accomplishment of
the elementary steps which contribute to Mastership. With the freshness of a new enterprise, you
are urged to remember that you are to be a guardian of the threshold. All the awakened pupils on
earth must be watchmen for the Christ Hierarchy,
signalers between the two worlds—belonging to
neither, yet a part of both.

When your basic endeavors are completed, then
you are ready for this step: Beginning once more
with the alignment technique, you will then reverently command each body's atomic intelligences
to be flooded by their joyous reception of the Light.

From this beginning you proceed to the second
stage. With every body in order, with integration
established, and with humility which tempers, har-
monizes, purifies the entire self, you do what might
be called your watchman labor. Begin by clearing

123

aside your psychic enclosures. Not only are men and women imprisoned by their own auras which include deterrent forces, but they are likewise surrounded by other heavy atmospheres which do not move until they are ordered or worked upon or changed by definite minds and wills. Moreover, the beneficent energies and gleaming archetypes which could motivate sincere aspirants of earth often go undetected because of those forces which act as barriers in the etheric, astral and mental planes.

It is necessary now for you to become a wielder of the Light. As a watchman, stand tall spiritually and let the stature of your inner might, beauty, nobility, and the totality of your gathered powers enable you to be a commanding, watchful spokesman. First, give the reverent command for your aura to be cleansed by God Light. Then see the stream as moving from the crown chakra in your head down to areas below your feet, and then moving upward from the left side of your body to the crown center once again.

After you have sensed the clearing of your auric orbit, you next extend and widen the circle of atmosphere about you. This will cause a momentary enlargement of your aura. It will again recede to its former proportions unless you remember to keep a wide influence, an ever-increasing and active field around you.

Next your efforts will be directed to the etheric forces which constitute the adjacent plane with which you must deal. After you sense clearing and widening in that region, work to open up and broaden your contact with the astral realm with which you are familiar. Make a pathway through spiritual will and through the vigor of your inward command by saying, *"Let the path be one of Light, and let there be openings!"* Likewise, make an inner, willful determination to see that your auric forces do open up the atmosphere about you and keep it clear until you can widen it still further.

Move on to the lower mental region. It is in this area that a great deal of clarification must take place since this is where most persons are burdened by all that they carry around within their brooding minds. You must not only purify your mind and let go of all the negatives and darkness, unhappiness and frustration that would impinge, but you may and must through such clearings allow the analytical powers of the mind to become one with the creative aspects of consciousness, until the mind is unified. Remember again to practice awareness and observation for this exercise purifies the mental vehicle. Afterwards, with a resolute mind a pathway is opened up in the mental region, and at last in the creative causal region, followed by the Adonaic. Finally, one does not try to open up a pathway to Absolute Spirit; one simply dwells within the conscious expanding powers of the God Flame.

After this work is accomplished, you will then concentrate on your home in the same manner, purifying, raising and enlarging the auric bands around it. Then you will work upon your neighborhood or area of residence, after which you may begin to work upon your planet as a whole in just this way.

When at last you come to the alchemical work of spirit done for your planetary world, you should take one aspect at a time, giving one day to it, and working at two-hour intervals. Begin this planetary purification with the physical world, and ask that light of the impressive, vibrant, transforming kind with thermal intensity become expressive in the physical world over the areas of world tension and unrest first, then your own United States, and finally all the other countries involved in the current conflict and battle of wills.

You should ask for the psychic debris, the vortexes of physical violence to be attacked by Light and given Light's antiseptic cleansing. On the following day, you should do the same work from the etheric level knowing that in this region your vortexes are larger and more fluidic and less responsive than those on the physical plane.

Then you climb to the astral conception of these vortexes of so-called evil. There you work to have cleared not only the amalgamation forces that be-set the violence, but all the individuals involved with the conflict, voluntarily and involuntarily, so that their astral forms are purified and cleansed of evil intent.

Climb to the mental region which is less respon-sive still and take a longer time for treatment. There you work upon the vortexes being cleared so that they do not feed evil in men and do not nour-ish their low imaginations to the greater creation of horrors. Clear out, as best you can, just as you have been instructed to do in regard to your own edam atomic rings, the tendency to react with thoughts from lower motivations.

Continue this cleansing treatment by asking that all these centers of psychic distress and disease re-ceive the new impulses which must come by invi-tation and by inroads made for them from the higher levels to cleanse the evil thoughts and their effects on every plane. Let the new energies come forth, invite them, summon them in reverence, make the command that there be clearings. If you cannot sense any clearing, then do the work of opening yourself, envisioning pathways by which Divine beams may enter to do their re-creative work and to effect the new releasements of wisdom for the guidance of your world leaders.

This gives you a simple idea of how you as a watchman can take your place and accomplish

127

your own service for the Christ Hierarchy and for
the world.

It is suggested that you simplify your living
habits and food choices to such an extent that
power can be generated from your wiser living.
Beginning on a chosen day, at the even two-hour
intervals, you are directed to again practice how
to govern the atomic structure of your total beinghood. You are especially urged to add to every
vehicle's treatment your will to throw off the sedi-
ment and negative encumbrances which burden
your various bodies.

On the second day at two-hour periods, this time
the uneven periods, you are urged to do special
work upon the cleansing of your emotional or astral form. First, during the morning hours make a
vigorous attempt to release from your astral body
all the stored impressions gathered negatively since
early childhood. Face them, release them, and be
finished with all these emotionally clinging forms.
During your afternoon periods invite new habits,
new desires and emotions of a definitely constructive order. Impress with will and reverence these
higher emotions upon the atomic intelligences of
your astral vehicle. In the evening, listen to music
of a lofty kind and allow the music to flood your
astral consciousness with its own cleansing and
uplifting influence.

On the third day, at the even two-hour intervals, practice fasting mentally from all emotions and thoughts of a destructive, death-giving kind. Expel, release and liberate from your mental bodies and from the edam ring of each atom the negative impurities and memories that are therein stored. During the afternoon on the even hours, welcome into your mental faculties thought frequencies that are elevating and restorative.

On another day, at the uneven hour intervals, work during the morning period to achieve greater awareness of the recesses of your Soul, and the consciousness of your inner individuality. Take time to become self-acquainted. During the afternoon, reverently command that the Individual Resident Within give forth to your conscious experience, days, and labors the enrichment and empowerment which It alone can yield. Ask for the orium band of the atoms composing your Causal Body to become open to and expressive of Divinity's frequencies.

These are the endeavors that will help to continue the good work and enable you more responsively to become aware. Live peacefully within yourself and powerfully through God indwelling you.

IF you would improve your concentration, this is a suggestion: Practice the stilling of the entire self. You must command your physical body to be still, as well as your energies and nervous impulses. Stillness, when commanded in the emotional nature, means restfulness and purity in that department. It is mental stillness, which amounts to an emptying, a draining out of your own human thoughts, which now requires your greatest effort. When the mind is perfectly calm, open and emptied of the negatives with which it might have been filled, then it is a mirror for the Soul to work upon and reflect through from its own superior height.

When you are attentive to the purpose of your concentrations, you will quiet yourself and liberate yourself in order that, through emptying, you can be filled from the eternal wellsprings of Spirit. The mind, therefore, will contain the objective of attention to the Real. The Soul will be in control of the whole man and yet will, as sentinel, point to the Everlasting. There is good reason for being quiet and attentive. The reason is attunement to the threshold of God-consciousness.

Remind yourself frequently of your reason, and let the door open of itself to release its power.

POSIT your thought and compass it by the good. Now you know from whence are to be born your courage and your strength. It rises not from dead things, nor from association with those who are not alive and who are only existing amidst the dreary valley of their twilight reflections. Your strength comes from immortal heights and from living Intelligences who again are only reflectors of that which They see with undimmed vision and receive with unceasing flow.

Carrots are not to be taken from mulberry trees, and birds are not found creeping through the slime of earth. That which is to be taken from the earth and that which is to be mastered on earth must be discovered and perfected in your spheres. The higher and the more spiritual realities come to you not by digging but by perceiving and by learning to climb and ascend to levels where they reside in power.

It may be of help to describe for you a student who was confused by the muchness of the sacred Truths. He ardently wanted, with perfection, the Holy Writ described. His life became a confusing series of applying this principle one day, and that application a following day, and giving realization to another value on a third day. He ended his incarnation with only a composite of muddied colors to show for his gain. Yet in the lives previous his entrance into the higher spheres resulted only in grayness. He will come in again and will think deeply and profoundly on all the elements revealed to him. From each he will extract an essence or a seed which shall be cared for and remembered deliberately and faithfully. He shall not then put

131

aside one Truth for another through the series of days. He shall complete in living remembrance and in worthy action all these recoveries of truths which he has been helped to witness.

These thoughts are shared with you for your study and intimate reflection.

To be more prosperous from the spiritual standpoint, it is needful to have an objective faith which is fully matched by wise action. See your need in each case for bringing through into your own existence the growth of *realized prosperity*. The gifts of Eternal Spirit are ever around you. It is needful that your individual television capture their images. That many will receive the same picture at one time is proof of the exhaustlessness of the *sending station*. In higher terms, the station does not need rehearsals. It never runs out of supply. Its characters for the distribution of means are constantly serving. You have to find a way in which to become more active with the goal of increased supply. It is right and trustworthy to expect the grace of unending provision. However, there are earlier stages where one's own talents and capacities for earning must be utilized. The surrounding Eternal will supply the strength, incentives, ideas and directives which must find an eager, enthusiastic, responsive agent in each who wishes to be prospered.

Keep the attention on prospering for a given goal, which in many cases should be an enlarged giving to Christ's Work. To neglect any medium through which able action can be taken in order to earn more is to be guilty of an offense of the evasions which prohibit right use.

Just as your health can be improved by your diligence and fidelity to practice without excuses and without disobedience, so can you as a person continue to improve in development along lines of spiritual purposefulness.

Meditate upon your temperament's quickening of the reception of ideas, of energies, and of spiritual joys. In your meditation work, particularly the first remembrance of the daytime, condition your body, your nerves, your entire vehicle of consciousness to the realization of quickening. In this morning period recall that you want to act more speedily, speak more inspiredly, and do all that you can to verify your own prayers, for the power will be there for your use as you ask for it.

Next, think of spiritual, holy joy—the joy God knows in creation—the joy the Brotherhood of Perfected Souls feels for even one conquest of a major kind in a human being. Reflect upon the joy which is exchanged in human hearts through unselfish love. Think of the joy of strangely comical human episodes. Every day think more of joy as a holy

133

gift of God to man. Meditate so strongly upon this theme that even though you might experience a spiritual testing, you would be so attuned to holy joy that it would be the current flowing through in the midst of your testing. Its light would feed your consciousness with thanksgiving thoughts—with power and shared words.

Third, at night do not retire at such a time that you are too exhausted for meditation or for sleep. One or two nights per month of late retirement would be allowable; but for the most part, retire sufficiently early that in your bedroom you can have a stilling, refreshing reflection. In your reflection period at this late hour tell yourself, *"I am a growing son or daughter of God. I have much to do both in the day and at night toward my growth. I desire to advance along lines that my meditations promise to program. I choose to meet my days joyously, with constructive faith, and with the quickening of spiritual powers. My days—all of them—shall be blessed with Light. My nights shall know the solemnity of good, deep rest. I choose to be at peace wherever I function and in whatever I do. This peace I know flows from God and feeds me in every moment with its kindly encouragement and sustainment."*

ALL that you face can be conquered through one channel—that of Divine Trust. Nothing facing you is as great or as serious as your fears and anxiousness make them. Strive diligently toward eliminating tension. That is your secret foe. Concentrate upon the constructives. Be open to the waves of God; and remembering to dwell in the Light consciously, tremors of the darkness shall no longer engulf you.

ONE OF THE WISE AND THE STRONG   BY ARTHUR G. LEARNED

STEWARDSHIP OF TIME

May the pearls of your hours indeed be enumerated and scrutinized with appreciative intent that the luster of their beauty and the value of their treasure shall be deeply known.

You must find for yourself a new ordering of life. It has been said that order is heaven's first law. Without the discipline of your mind, emotions and motivations, your energies are scattered. Therefore, conceive, day by day, a well-knit plan. Garner together your objectives, your stewardship of time and vitalities. Execute that for which your plan allows, though it keep you beyond midnight to attain it. Thereafter you will be wiser for observing your mistaken ambitions. The following day will find your plans more modest and in proportion to your stewardship of time and means for action.

TIME must be measured in your life. You are urged, therefore, to make an interior plan within your mind as to the execution of time within your allotment of conscious waking hours. If you have twenty tasks and three of them can be completed with excellence of conduct and quality of effort within one hour, the remaining seventeen can be performed one at a time, or again brought to accomplishment in twos or threes within an hour. Work not for haste, but for accomplishment. Be less mindful of the crowding of the many duties, but more thoughtful of the total sum that must be executed within one planetary day.

You are held responsible for the wiser and the better fulfillment of your duties in an earlier period of cancellation than you were accustomed to carry them out in previous times. Speak less to others aloud that you may think more about how to talk to them effectively. Sit quietly, planning the one-pointed execution of your tasks and waste no energy in needless motion or the flurry of nervous excitement. Heighten your mental powers and sharpen your sensibilities by recollection of the fact that energies will flow to you from space itself to energize and accomplish that which you conceive. Out of your twenty duties, aspire to make it a rule to fulfill twelve of them between the morning and noontime so that in the afternoon hours those assignments which require less conscious reflection may occupy your labors. The numerical equations which are suggested are to be thought of as generalities and not as specifics.

Those who are gentle are urged to become strong and forceful and positive. You must summon up from the interior of your own solar powers the depth of decisiveness. This positiveness of tone can only accelerate the happenings which you bring into being by your allowing them expression in your physical world through your audible powers.

Those who are positive and who are aware of unbalanced aggressiveness are given the charge to surrender the imbalances. Never forego the positiveness of deliberation from your Soul's level, but forego the strong rhythm—the tumultuous energy which accompanies such ardor of expression. Be decisive within and act out your decisiveness by taming the outer to be gentler, to be mild, reserved, an exponent of the Lord Christ's influence, one working from behind the scenes quietly, possibly unnoticed, but actively in tune.

You who are gentle must assert your positiveness and become the carriers of Divine Will among those who are surprised by your sudden announcements; and you who are too assertive must learn to be identified with the company of those who serve quietly and are not known. It is good to belong to a company of those who do not require praise or attention or credit.

TIME seems very fleet in your dimension, but the aspirations of your innermost self require the works of eternity. You must have infinite patience and a faith which is active in every moment. Too easily you glide over details and specifics with the

139

excuse that you are fulfilling generalities. It is these very missing marks, these slips from the conquest of the moment by moment work that are your most serious failures. Build gradually, but consciously, every waking moment.

PREPARE yourself more effectively in this fertile now. Arouse yourself from your lethargy of wasted hours. You must make good time. Learn to organize, perfect and brighten your own improvements in a unified manner. Persevere, be thorough; and even though you may be slow, remember that it is the quality of effort, not the quantity of achievement which is important at this time.

Your hours are short. Eternity is long. You must reconcile the two. Your thoughts and spirit can match the bliss and unity of the Eternal, even in your time-restricted dimension, for your affiliation with Eternity blesses you with Its immeasurable power.

WHAT VALUE lies in the powers of discrimination and good use of time! Your living needs to be divided in such a manner as to provide time for worship, work and ease of living—also time allotted for study. It is essential to approach your days with the reverence that can contain volumes of joyousness. No one else can determine the divisions you must arrange in your time-space world.

You are merely reminded to move toward a more intelligent distribution and wiser use of your daily hours.

Do NOT IDLE. These acts of your own devotions are openings through which the clarity of the higher spheres may flow to you. Your times of at-one-ment with the world of God and the Spirit of His Presence must each one be a holy adventure. Do not lag in other things; do not turn and look behind you toward the shadows that have ensnared too long your pilgrimage. Move on into the clear light of your own determined Soul's highlands. According to your approach to each period, according to the tenacity of your desire for thoroughness and the excellent execution of the command of spirit, shall be your reward of transformations.

AT THIS POINT in your instruction, you are urged to become *dedicated stewards of time.* Endeavor to learn how very wealthy you are in the resources of hours. Eliminate spendthriftiness. Do not give precious hours to circumstances, persons or activities that will be in themselves of no consequence. Learn to turn sharp, measured reasoning upon each new day so that the wide sweep of the hours will be appreciated and likewise properly consecrated in your meditations. It is essential to learn the conquest of procrastination. Recall unceasingly to tune

141

into the Soul's forces of attuned rhythms, and do your work through remembering contacts with Soulic chargings. Be more mindful of your duties and of how each task must be completed in a certain hour and not two hours hence. When the end of the day comes, leave your desk or task with a clear mind and go to other labors that are recreational.

Instruct yourself to keep on measuring the hours with valued use, making every word, every act and motive consciously bathed by Soulic anointing.

RELATEDNESS

There is no magic to equal Love's transcendent qualities. There is no problem which Love cannot help to answer.

LET your love be expressed to one another through highest action. Let your love be spiritual in nature, for when it is thus, it places no expectation upon the loved. But it looks deep into the heart and accepts without repulsion or condemnation the mistakes of what has many times been the evil past. This spiritual love likewise enlivens the fires of growth and through goodwill nourishes the brother's desires for unfoldment.

It is a requisite for those who are beginning to touch Eternal Life while still in their human encasements to love all in such a way that humanity itself is given insight into the love of the Spirit for man. In your higher bodies you observe each other with deepest and highest approval and with gratitude that your lives were linked. Let the realization which is true and active in the inner worlds now become a part of your outer regard *for all*. Do not be automatons or so purely primitive that you love only those who belong to you. Live according to the height of your best spiritual advances, for from this height you will regard each one—every single member of humanity—as exceedingly important and valuable to existence. Break down and overcome your commonplace acceptance of others. As you may have known, every human soul has within him a *jewel* that no one, except his inner Instructors, has discovered. Sometimes glimpses of this jewel shine through the personality self, but more often it is so heavily veiled, so encrusted by the failures of living that the jewel's priceless Light remains hidden.

Those who serve the Lord and who walk in the way of spiritual knowingness must be intelligent miners, using sincere and ever-deepening methods for finding access to that jewel in every person's being. You are impoverished until you find it, not only in yourself, but in your brothers. When you have found this special and unique spiritual aspect of greatness in your brother, his *real self* shall always be your benefactor. Take nothing for granted as to whether or not your brothers or sisters are happy, well, able to live adequately. Investigate through your own heart's promptings methods for assisting them to a greater degree of peace and freedom.

CONSIDER these points of importance to discipleship and growth:

For some, there is the question of how to meet

opposition and positivity in others. First, such testings come as a result either of complete failure to
subdue one's own positivity or from needing to
awaken to an exercise of one's own will. Persons
who are themselves most positive are prone to try
others who are similar. For that reason, perceiving
the nature of this testing to be one of creating an
unpleasant disturbance of equilibrium, be watchful for any and every opportunity to conquer your
own inner reaction. In the beginning it is imperative to concentrate upon your own maintenance of
right attitude. With your advancement in control
and imperviousness, the other person's discordant
reaction may then be treated. When angry, fearful, uphappy or upset, one's energy gushes forth
in exaggerated momentum from the astral body.
Were this state of agitation allowed to persist over
too long a period, insanity or death would follow.

Realizing that a willful, dictatorial, or simply a
more positive attitude in another can be the means
of trial, determine that with the first, as well as
with every onslaught of this form of testing, you
will immediately neutralize the emotions and with
spiritual will insulate the aura. As long as one does
not feel the same type of current that the offender
feels, one has advantage. Therefore, it is not well
to allow oneself even to become angry, for then
your antagonist has the advantage. Righteous in-
dignation in the face of evil is justified, but indig-

nation over trivials begets unwholesomeness. The Soul, thinking, loving and guiding the experience from above can give the devotee impressions of the relative merits of the situation. Therefore, to silence positivity which is offensive in another, one must speak words of firmness, but without any degree of discordant emotion—not even with the feeling of superiority.

Again, using spiritual strategy, there are occasions when in truth a "soft answer turneth away wrath." Gentleness, with firmness and love, is healing and enlightening to the testing one. In unpleasant moments, one must feel and think, *"This falls away from me. I shake it loose from my vehicles and through God's Light it is expelled from my orbit and surrendered to God treatment."*

IF LOVE is sterile in your heart you are not only lonely, but very incomplete and short-circuited in alignment to power. Frequently recall these words as you build pathways between your heart and the hearts of others. You are singly responsible for making model relationships. You may hate, despise and oppose sin or evil, but you may never so regard persons. Only when you are sure a friend or foe travels the left-hand path of evolution may you accord him indifference most purposefully. Indifference, rather than hate, hurts the followers of the left-hand path, the testers of humanity.

146

More importantly, establish between yourself and others, strong, pure and unfailing connectives. Begin to work upon your model of improved relationships with those closest to you at this time. Build up a wondrous connective with the Soul of your nearest and most intimate brothers and sisters. With them, exercise Christ sisterhood and brotherhood. Knowing their weaknesses, you must more gently, and on occasion more firmly, outpicture the trust, respect and treatment you would accord them if they were entirely free from those weaknesses. How can someone, torn and bleeding in his emotional body, know what peace is like unless someone shines out to him the emanations and radiations which are quieting and healing?

You need to be busier in the use of experimental processes for the harmonizing and the perfecting of your husbandry, your wifehood, your sisterhood, brotherhood and friendship. As long as you permit echoes, canyons, and deep lakes of dark powers to exist between you and others you are not fulfilling your obligation toward spiritual relationships.

Do not excuse yourself. You might have been unruly, discordant and very unloving for a long time. Today you might be a bundle of destructive nuclei because you are uncomfortable and poisoned by your own unloving attitude. You have no right to extend your miserableness into the consciousness of another. Bear your griefs, your frus-

147

trations, your illnesses, your discontents with better dignity of spirit. Let your negativity cease within yourself. To others reflect a light—the light of your goodwill, your appreciation, cooperation, patience, and above all, your spiritual love.

Surely among the brotherhood of conscious devotees and aspirants, love must not fail. Love needs to gladden, refine, fill with peace, and deepen with respect the many to whom it is given as a priceless gift. When you exercise the best of your faith and reverence, you will not fail the Lord Christ. It is equally important that you never fail each other.

You are as islands on the sea of ignorance. Your heads are lifted above the dark waters toward the unending sky and the star connectives. Call to one another from your individual islands in purest harmony. Then shall your island of individuality rise until its mountainous proportions become visible.

LOVE, with all its wonderment, is still to be experienced more perfectly in your practice of discipleship training. If love is present in the heart and in the Soul, God's Spirit Indwelling *is* functioning. This becomes one of your deepest needs.

To live in love forever, to achieve the beginning of this advanced realization, you can begin with the simple desire or prayer to live, to feel, and to broadcast love from your very Soul. Since any objective that is related to causal realities requires depth, thoroughness and love for God, be reminded of the necessity for conditioning your approach to love from your Soul Self. Let those who love only a few, determine this year to love many. Let those whose personality mannerisms are contrary to love, refine, soften and melt their brusqueness and their poor self-management with the end in view of love's generous outpouring through their kindliness, their thoughts, and through their chastened conduct.

Let the self-willed and the self-centered desire a greater love—the love of the Supreme Spirit—for as many as can be discovered as lovable. The necessary self-giving, as a gift of love to others, will be a bright present made observable to all those who have a right to be interested in this soul's growth.

Let the surface thinkers and the shallow-hearted concentrate this year upon deepening love, sympathy and interest in others. Let those who love easily and inclusively learn to love more wisely still.

Let those who are troubled by their rejection of the unloving remember to place such persons in God's all-wise care with the deepest yearning for their inner transformation.

Love shall make the lonely content and at peace. Love shall give the unrefined the mellowing of Christliness. Love shall give the empty, hollow-hearted, genuine worth. Love shall give the neurotic healing and new self-development of a kind

149

which is unselfish. There is no quality that can excel love or exceed its quickening power. Greater than wisdom in its effectiveness and its blessedness, love is the beginning and the end of all human needs.

Take heart! Keep the faith! Rely on those powers which shall bring you more readily, and always and unfailingly, to the fulfillment of discipleship's quest. In the name of the Lordly One, the Hierarch Christ, you are ensouled and entered by love. Keep true to the majesty of its sovereign power.

LOVE one another and all that is a part of your way of life with the love of spiritual beholding. Recognize the work of Christ as the ideal brotherhood and lend your powers toward that attainment among your fellowmen with expressed Christ love for all. Each day promise yourself to help the one who is offensive and give him the assistance of your truth-bringing observation and the recognition of your trust in his ability to become regenerate.

Through love of others, and especially for the Cause of Christ, seek daily opportunities to put love into action so that through self-forgetting interest in others the blessings of love may begin their transformations. Concentrate in meditations at intervals upon the unloved persons of your group and of society's family, and send forth your beam of love's inclusion to them. Let these remembrances stir within you a desire to bring relief, change, freedom and happiness to those persons. Be not ensnared or entangled by the perversions of human instincts, misnamed love. Whenever and wherever you can, correct, bring to light, and cleanse within yourself and other persons these perverted forces. Right your relationships through the quality and the standard of pure and deep Christ love for the Souls of all men.

ONE OF THE WISE AND THE STRONG   BY ARTHUR G. LEARNED

SPIRITUAL ASPECTS OF HEALTH

Through contact with innermost God, one by one the tentacles of the destructive instinctive nature will be loosed—and permanently.

HEALING to be permanent must flow from God Within. For those who require healing it is vital to relax while contemplating God Indwelling. When well, it is wisest to build fortifications of inner strengthening. However, in the event of sickness the same procedure may be used with benefit. Contemplate the Self of Light within you. When an awareness of the best concentration possible is realized, ask then for a release of the shedding of Light.

Realize that the Light of God is the sustainer of life. Contemplate the release of Light energies into and through all the faculties and systems of being. The Light, through your asking, can reach the mental body and activate the positive potentials of your thinking to the extent that you develop new convictions of the health of mind and attitudes.

As the Light shedding continues and the splendor of Divinity centers upon the feeling self, enjoy feelings of peace that are supplied by the Light of

God Within. On this level allow waves of depression, resistance and aggression, as well as rebellion and fear, to flow into the Light's presence and into its commitment.

Let the sunlight radiations center upon, throughout and around human energies. Submit your energies willingly and as completely as possible to the Light's healing and enlivenment. Permit God's solar force to center upon those organs whose vibrations have become slow, devitalized and demagnetized. Do not cease to focus the beam of the sunlight of Spirit upon the organ until a degree of warmth and peace and relaxation is sensed.

Now ask that an active stream of God currents energize the entire physical vestment, reattuning every organ, recharging the cells, and filling to overflow the aura around yourself or the person for whom this vitalizing work is done.

Were men to remember to employ the forces of God within them, a perpetual season of peaceful well-being would exist.

EVERYONE needs to build about himself an armor which no assailant nor catastrophe may destroy. This armor is called *peace*. All that you take into the household of your own consciousness must be conditioned by this inward peace. The elements of which your various relationships are composed must be divested of their opposites and only their

154

likeness to and agreement with peace must remain. Permit no disappointment, challenge, fear or joy to rob you of your peace, but take these various visitors into the household of your being and see how nearly they can be changed through the radiations of peace that are poured upon them. Those which are imposters and do not belong in the house of your being must consciously be expelled when once their negativity appears unchangeable. You need to know that whatever you fear—that which has not been changed into a peaceful acceptance within consciousness and has not been fully expelled from your attention—will lie in the courtyard of your being, gathering momentum, until power sufficient is exercised for their transmutation into the Light. *No man or woman or circumstance should be allowed to take your peace from you;* but most of these things you meet as tests, if they are rightly accepted into your own household, they will no longer be strangers or opponents—but will be friends.

It is needful that you consider the alchemical influence of love in the work of healing. You need to be so in love with God that everything is viewed in proper balance. Through complete love of Divinity, the needs of others, the beauty of others, and of the little things and creatures will be placed before the self. Were you able to live these tenets of profound spiritual importance, the obstructions

155

within the self would be melted by the wholeness of this wider sight.

Occasionally the instinctive nature will incite a threatening storm, an inundation of unmastered forces. All the fears, resistance, conflicts and rejections that have been temporarily buried will arise as a tidal wave, and in the most apparently insignificant situation reveal their titanic presences. It is these uprisings, though unnoticed by other persons, which darken the aura, deplete the inward vehicles, and cut off the powers of replenishment that feed man's inner self. During these uprisings of criticism, doubt and rebellion he should allow the quality and the baptism of love from the Soul self to saturate, cleanse, pacify and release these inward storms. If you will take a resistant thought consciously into the presence of the love within the center of your being, you will have more than enough impetus, ability and energy with which to change, transform and heal the negative, enemy factors within your household. Remember that all these unpleasant hosts which your consciousness has harbored unknowingly for centuries of time *can be changed in the vibrancy of one moment* if you will love unselfishly, unstintingly, purely and compassionately from the altitude of your Soul.

Love is the breath, the beauty, and the wisdom of the Soul, and on no other lower plane does love exist; but love can be sent down into the lesser regions of consciousness when permitted and when invited.

Persons who achieve rebirth and who attain a releasement of factors that contributed to their ill health and to their sickness of mind, can be transfigured and released permanently from the enemies within their own households by love's baptism which makes a brother of an opponent and a co-worker of an assailant.

Let there be search toward discovery of the inward meaning of this lesson as it applies to your individual life and to the changing and transfiguring of all your difficulties through love.

It is needful that you comprehend the inner side of healing because of its significance in relation to complete physical well being and wholeness. An individual might do all the proper outward things in regard to excellent physical care and the wise choice and preparation of foods, without achieving health. The inside of man, his psychological development, and his moral and spiritual departments require as great, *if not greater*, remembrance and care. Many times a person becomes ill even while living wisely in the outward sense, simply because he cannot stand the stresses, pressures, and entangling subtleties and currents that his sensitive nature encounters. For that reason he must assume as vigilant a control and command of his

157

inward life as he has learned to assume without.

It was mentioned earlier that the two cardinal requisites by which the inward nature must be regulated and ordered are those of an expression of unceasing peace, plus the living of love from deep within. What you can forgive and what you can love can have no adverse or harmful effect upon you. Therefore, to your strongest assailants, and to those who would destroy you even unknowingly by the vampirism of their negative habits, you need to bring defeat with constructive powers and principles. You need to prevent them from hurting you further.

When your own insulation is well enough established, their negativity will rebound to them rapidly and forcefully and they will begin to see what they are like as others view them. Then they are themselves ready for healing and they will have to approach wholeness in the same manner by which their older and higher brother, sister, helpmate and kin have done.

Today you are reminded to bring into use a third factor which is called *decisive self-control.* Reflect frequently in your intervals of remembrance that the creativity of your own mind, as well as all the powers of consciousness which comprise your being, need to be brought to a recognition of a superior and a creative command.

It is easy, when once you are disciplined, to be at

peace and to be loving, forgiving and constructive in your regard toward others. But this alone would not protect you. You need, from the center of yourself, with yourself actually in command, to have one constructive, motivating, energizing and radiating idea that will act as your pilot and will wield the insulating forces you require for your greater God-protection. Never permit another, unless he be superior to yourself in growth, to influence you from the center of yourself. Let the resident and regent thought to which you persistently hold be: *"I am in command of my life and my circumstances. My command is open to the instruction as well as the supervision of God Who is supreme. In this thought of self-possession and self-direction, I broadcast to every cell, faculty and department of my being, my will which is God's Will, for my unfettered growth."* Substitute statements of this kind with those which more adequately suit your own temperament and needs. *Express the realization that you are in charge and nothing which is false, lowering or fearful may rule or decide in opposition to your inward welfare.* This of course would be extreme if carried minutely into all relationships. The element of decisive self-control and of positive will must be active in those who have been troubled by illness so that their aura is clearly and energetically a radiating center rather than a passive one afflicted by the vampirism of

the fears, attachments and possessions of those who
are as yet not completely given to the inward life
of consecration.

WORLD TREATMENT

Every disciple needs to be a vessel for the healing of the world.

"THOU Who art God, send forth Thy powers in streams and in bombardments into mankind's total awareness. Let the Will of Peace be the compass guiding every man and every nation's heart. Send Thy forces of strenuous, potent activity into all the areas, hosts, governments and persons who oppose the Light of Brotherhood's progress. Enable the God-loving and highly motivated members of the earth to become custodians of Thy Will for permanent and invincible Peace in, upon and throughout this planet. In the name of the Lord Christ who is powerfully present and centered in the earth, so let this be!"

IT IS IMPORTANT to clarify in your mind what is taking place in the inner worlds in relation to the mortal combat now in embattlement between the God-reverencing world and the ideology of communism. Up to this time the battle has been largely an astral and a physical contest. Now, however, the two powerful contestants are lining up more definitely. On the inward side and from this period

161

forward the contest will include more than ever before, the mental dimension.

In the past there has been a gradual increase in awareness of how sharply divided the two opposing companies are perceptively. At present nearly every adult is called upon to declare his position and work decisively within the ranks of his choice. Since communism associates with the dark forces or left-hand stream of consciousness, it is expedient that everyone, who to any degree worships the Divine God, bring himself as a completely pledged soldier, willing and trained by inward means to do individual battle with the opposing army. What this refers to is the need for more extensive and more persistent use of inner plane methods and work in your labors for your side. Beginning now, it should be every man's covenant to relate himself more positively to Christ's company and to strive through God Love to use constructive means for wiping out infestations of darkness.

The spearhead of your advance must be through regular, effectual and wise prayers and remembrance periods. Realizing some of the weaknesses of the dark assailants, you will be better informed and enabled to make your spearhead's thrust felt with might. Those who are open to an ever-extending degree to the supreme reality of God are greatly influenced by the Divine Outflow upon the levels which are subjective. This involuntary side, which relates them to Divine Response, begins in their Spirit and is correspondingly and simultaneously engendered within the Soul and its levels, and the astral body and its planes, and the instinctive areas of being. Man would be more like the Angels were his positivity active in this subjective side of individuality.

It happens instead that human beings are more cultivated in their objective faculties than in the subjective ones. The objective faculties are related to will, mind and physical body.

At man's unity with God-consciousness at illumination, the seven branches of being are equalized. The assailants who would entice the society of mankind and give them a world government completely lacking in God-direction, function primarily upon the planes of will, mind, and physical force. They are strongest in these branches, even as the company on the side of God who oppose them are more to be found energizing the subjective faculties and instruments of the self.

Until the armies of God's people are as forceful on all planes as their opponents are on three planes, they will meet with frustrations and with the experience of simply holding the enemy at bay. Each man of God must learn how to spearhead the Light of constructive opposition against the black waves of ungodliness.

Each of you should become vitally interested in

163

the successful outcome on the side of Light of every
United Nations' important decision. Your government's affairs and dealings with other countries
should receive your treatments and your strongest
prayers. Before each high noon remembrance period of world needs, ask that the Divine Spirit Who
is active within endow the will of your being and
the will of all on the side of the company of Light
with wholesome, dominant force through the positive Will of Peace. See to it that the Soul supplies
the mind of not only your own being but of those
who stand for the same cause you serve, with ever-
renewing, vital and interesting thoughts that can
be employed as weapons by God's agents of Light.

Let benevolent, pure and unselfish feeling govern and train the instincts of your own self and
those of others in the world around you. See all of
this work as an endeavor within the company of
God-loving humanity whose motivation is to can-
cel out and to master the darkness, so that the
goodwill for peace shall be manifest in every government and in all the peoples of earth.

THOSE who volunteer to assist in prayer cordon
world treatment work often ask how they might
make their individual prayer periods of greatest
possible service. Here are a few suggestions:

You should have a day prior to your time of vigil
for the alerting of your faculties, for summing up

your spiritual energies—a day given to the remembrance of dwelling within the Presence of the
Eternal World.

When your period of prayer comes, open your
vigil with worship of the Christ. Greet Him as the
Hierarch of all spiritual efforts and attainment.
Ask that He use such ventures as this for more
completely entering His world.

Your second expression of this prayer will devote
itself to invoking the Christ Spirit to enter the
planet. You need to visualize this Spirit as a bright
Light that may enter particles of material or physical substances to make them more luminous, more
accelerated by spiritual frequencies.

Thirdly, it is well for you to concentrate upon the
Christ Spirit coming into the great body of mankind. For several minutes entertain the thought of
this mass body until it becomes dear to you and in-
tensely important. You will work by continents
rather than by nations, seeing the peoples of earth
as receptive to this Christ Element known as His
Spirit. You will realize as you pray for the peoples
of each continent that they consist of numerous be-
liefs, both religious and political. Ask that those
who are not Christians yet, be enkindled by the
love experience which is not found in other world
faiths. Treat for Catholicism to be entered in such
a way that the erroneous interpretations of literal
acceptances give way to more universal and expan-

165

sive realizations. Know that Protestantism with all its dividedness can come spiritually into a great body of unified reception to the Lord of Hosts. Recognize that there are many divergent forms of the Christ teachings which, from the most material to the most highly esoteric, require cleansing and activation by the vital Christ Element.

Then see the governments of the world as open to the influence, through the Lord Christ, of the Planetary's Will for world at-one-ment. Even as it is necessary for religions to lose their secular boundaries, so is it essential, even imperative, that the governments of the world cease their rigid nationalism, to enter a new state of true fellowship based upon spiritual brotherhood.

In your work you will ask that the powers— Godly and Angelic—capable of performing the necessary quickenings and transformations will act upon these world bodies in such a way that differences will not be permitted to remain partitions any longer. Strive once again to love this earth and its population with such depth that crime, war, disease, suffering and want are felt by your Soul. Then only, because of your sympathy and your realization, are you able to call down the victorious Christ Element, otherwise known as the Christ Spirit, that it may enter the places and persons on earth wherein these destructives are most prevalent.

Next, you will bring yourself, as one of the

166

whole of mankind who is willing, ready and receptive, to the incarnation of the Christ Spirit. Then
abide in attunement with this vast Presence in
worship. You will see it through your mental and
soulful processes as the alchemical force of Deity,
entering your being to refine, to bless, to hasten,
and to redeem sluggish activations. You will see
that the conflict between the Spirit's urge to be vig-
orously active and the earth's material essences
which are rebellious and inclined to indulgence,
formulates a pact, a unity and a marriage in which
the higher essences from the Spirit within are permitted leadership.

Should you do your work fully and from the
highest level of your Soul's aspiration, you will
have the mystic experience, which Masters abid-
ingly know, of being a conscious and very necessary part of humanity's growth and blessing.

WHEN you pray you need to be so completely in
agreement with the fiery currents of prayer that
all asking, all urging, even all inward impatience
is purified as the right form of prayer is uttered.
When you pray completely in tune with the realization of the Presence you address, there is no unpleasantness or lingering wonder left in you as to
the results of your prayer efforts. In positive prayer
you are conscious that the action is now taking
place and you are in its midst, and there is nothing

167

further you have to do except add to the prayer's potency by daily, positive workmanship on your part.

EXPERIENCES AFTER TRANSITION

*Not one moment passes but that the golden
flow from Eternity reaches your dimension.*

IT IS expedient that you comprehend the adjustments which take place after death in order that you can in your present abode meet some of their requirements. Fortunate are those persons who enter the larger regions having served Divine principles to the fullest of their ability while yet on earth.

The purpose of relating certain happenings to you is that you will realize your opportunity for making better use of Divine realities. At transition the one who is undergoing change is wholly conscious of the dynamic properties within the Light which are focused upon him. Although there are several and even at times a small group witnessing the change of the human being, their nearness is obscured by the greater, full-orbed brilliance of the releasing Light. This Light usually persists in its one-pointed focus until the memorial service has been completed. After this occasion, the one who has undergone transition is able to see the new world and its residents who are about him.

During the three days of his body's rest prior to

the memorial event he had undergone the cleansing and the strengthening of the pools. Usually
this is experienced without conscious recognition.
Perhaps the first impression the newly arrived individual receives concerning those who meet him
is his perception of images and obscurations which
exist between him and those beheld. He perceives
that the others are not troubled by these images.
Gradually he knows they do not see what he does.
Between those loved and the beholder are astral
substances which were formed by the human being
in his distorted or untrue or exaggerated regard
of those who were once around him. These astral
images can be likened to poorly constructed masks
that are seen midway between the beholder and
those who highly regard him. Occasionally the
substance takes the form of veils or even of hanging
moss-like creations that exist midway between
himself and another.

No one tells him what these disorderly impressions are. Gradually he learns from resources within that these are misconceptions and the prejudiced
views he has falsely held concerning those whose
impressions they do not fit. Thus the first lesson
for the newly arrived is one of slowly, sincerely
and without prejudice endeavoring to learn what
persons are really like.

Finally these mirages clear and the beholder dis-
covers in the dimension of emotion a stronger fond-

ness and a wider arc of appreciation than was true of him in the outer world due to the limitations of his consciousness.

The second discovery is that of wonder, filled with degrees of awe for the beauty and the lucid clarity of loved persons, Souls and thoughts. The human being at last appreciates the value of greater silence, for this enables him to perceive and to gain wise judgments regarding the true and fine qualities possessed by former human members.

In a similar manner this newly arrived one finds it best, as he advances, to have no preconceived notions regarding most things. After one has thoroughly absorbed enjoyment from re-established relationships and has been spiritually inspired by the perceived good in those who had preceded him, he comes to the state of desiring new conquests. This second period occupies what would be years in three dimensional time. Everyone senses the invigoration and stirring which his new-found freedom allows. Under this impetus, vocations, desires and unfulfilled yearnings are permitted encouragement or investigation. This is the period for exploration, comparable to travel in your world, for scientific studies, and for inventive pursuits. One may travel the length of his own solar system since all the planets and their sun have inner dimensional linking. This new-found pleasure has within it revelation not afforded on the earth. In quietness

171

and with studiousness one realizes the meaning of places, values, works, and even possibilities, from depth perception. Hence the beholder frequently desires to revisit sites and areas of his own globe that he may now study the place he formerly regarded with surface appreciation. The beholder now estimates the new colors and the particular qualities which are in effect in countries or within groups and institutions he wishes to investigate.

Always the thought recurs with emphatic pressure, *"Why, while on earth, was I so blind and insensitive and static! If only my attention had been free of self-interest, I might have found how more appropriately to become a server for the inflowing of special forces through the place or through this study."* With ever-improving receptiveness, the quester finds a desire to no longer follow his many longings, but he prefers instead to confine himself to sincere and thorough study. This gives him contact with the Halls of Learning. Having desire for specific information, he may require instruction in a subject which would deal with the work called, "From Realization to Application." His very desire for specialized knowledge leads him with clearest intuition into the very group and to the very teacher who are together responsible for this information. In these classes time does not intrude. For that reason the quester may continue in a given class for what would equal several days in three

172

dimensional time. There is no mental fatigue and no emotional tension within the higher worlds. Hence, teachers remain with a subject uninterruptedly until their pupils have understanding of the values revealed.

In the various classrooms, students again experience mirages floating before their sight, and in between the teacher and themselves, wherever the subject touches upon preconceived ideas on the student's part. Knowing now what these obscurations signify, the quester listens all the more purely and as his openness increases the images disappear. In classrooms, questers find instruction accorded them on more than one level. Some of these students are conscious that while on earth they might have been much more richly renewed and taught if they had listened really and purely without the shadow reflections of themselves intruding.

From these simple insights take heart, and with more deliberation apply yourself while yet in your human frame to receiving wisdom and to the reception of Divinity's Love broadcast without self-imposed restrictions. See without prejudice. Try to understand others as they are, not as you want to imagine or as your limited sight would distort your viewpoint. If you conquer in this outer dimension the obscurities that plague the limited, then in truth will the Kingdom's wisdom and beauty hallow your earth experience.

173

ONE OF THE WISE AND THE STRONG   BY ARTHUR G. LEARNED

PREPARATION FOR HOLY DAYS

Turn your thoughts to the infinitudes of Spirit and release your prayers upon Its oceans of Light.

IT IS always helpful in times of high spiritual tides to practice self-denial reverently. For that reason, during the forty-six days prior to Easter, deny yourself of physical destructives and also of the very traits you still possess which are obstacles to your own Easter experience. Perhaps indolence, selfishness, or disinterestedness in the concerns of others are so habitual that you are not conscious of their danger. For the forty-six days of Lent, work on these traits that these hindrances may be rolled away by the strong tides within your Spirit. If you are blind to your own chief detriments, ask those who know you best to suggest lovingly and frankly what they would deem advisable for you to transcend.

It is suggested that you devote these significant days prior to the monumental event of Easter to a complete and willing dedication and surrender to the work of the Lord. As a devotee of the Lord Christ, you should contribute your own lighted effort to His great cause.

During the full term of this spiritual event concentrate upon and consecrate yourself ever more lovingly, worshipfully and directly to the Lord of all religions earth knows. Out of this extended appreciation of and contact with the true Christ Hierarch will come accelerated impressions for your own deeper self-giving.

One of the ways by which you may serve the Christ Cause is to devote all of Lent to prayers for others. Certain conditions might necessitate your praying for your deepened channelship, for your improved development, or for your unfoldment of courage and wisdom. However, rather than concentrating upon endeavors for your own development, it would be preferable for you to devote these forty-six days to unselfish prayer and labor for other persons. Until mastership, self-emptying is a necessary and a beneficial accomplishment.

Pray every two hours during Lent for mankind's needs as a whole. During one period of your vigils, pray as if the burden of man's re-creation rested in part upon you. Put more love and more feeling into your words of address to the Eternal. The more greatly you love your sisters and brothers on earth, the stronger become the channeling powers by which Divinity seeks to heal and enlighten men.

In another period you might devote yourself each day with fresh enthusiasm to praying for those who need help through difficult phases of their advancement. This should include individuals to whom you are not particularly attracted.

In a third period you might work prayerfully for rays and frequencies of Light from the Angel Kingdom to enter earth's atmosphere for universal upliftment in particular areas of the world requiring spiritual aid.

Lift up before the attention of the Hierarchy all religions of the world in order that peoples of all faiths may be inwardly united in trust and mutual respect.

In the last remembrance period of your day recall the gathering forces of Eastertide. With stillness, with veneration and with faith, help these special Eastertide currents to bridge their assistance to humanity. Contemplate the outpouring of the Mysteries of the Godhead—the boundless glories which the Eternal channels. With reverence and with positive trust you will pray: *"Let the Eastertide come! Let Its currents heal the divisions and heartaches of nations and peoples! Let men be ready to walk the upward path of the mountain of their own mastership!"*

With Christmas, one of the greatest days of your calendar, six weeks away you have a wonderful preparatory period in which to rightly sensitize yourself for the coming of this festival. In fact, for

177

ages Adepts have encouraged their pupils to enter disciplines consisting of six weeks of time.

During the first week you should practice concentrating upon key qualities which are related to initiatory forces within this festival of rebirth. Beginning the first day, then, and continuing for one week, the suggested quality to accent is *peace.*

You can do your best each day of this week if you think creatively and resourcefully about the characteristics and powers of peace. Think this day about the peace of great things, such as the skies when they are tranquil, or the mountains and their serenity, or the ocean when peaceful, or a moonlit night. Let your own symbols of tranquility suggest themselves to you, and be receptive to constructive energies which flow from this exercise.

The fortitude, vigor and poise of mountains suggest an abiding patience, a patience that is vast and deep.

On a second day you could think of peaceful persons, starting with the Lord Christ, and then give your attention to great souls of the past as well as the present who embody this remarkable quality. At the conclusion of such a meditation you might repeat: *"I would that the Source of deep peace likewise enter me, to make me a channel of Its outflow."*

In this last statement is an idea for a third day of endeavoring. At various times during this purposeful day, allow your thoughts to review the attitudes of consciousness you practiced while attuned to the great Source of Peace itself—the everlasting Spirit, the active God, who moves in utter stillness and performs in serenest manner His works of creation.

On the fourth day you will think of your own inward center of peace which begins for you in your own Soul Self.

A time will come when, as an unfolded Master, your Soul will be wholly influenced by the Adonai; a higher expression of being which is responsible for the peace, energy, will and intelligence that you inherently embody.

Thus is outlined for you a way by which you might interestingly and earnestly vary your procedures of devotional thought each day. Christmas should be a freshet of inspiration to all consecrated Christians. If you prepare yourself inwardly with faith, following such instructions devotedly, you shall be at all times and in all places consciously overshadowed and safefolded.

Beginning the second week, meditations upon the characteristic of *self-control* would be most fitting for Christmastide preparation. Again seek symbols and thought images by which to direct your specific inner activities. Be eager to be inspiredly receptive to spiritual guidance from the higher levels of consciousness. Once more you will creatively ponder the meanings and values that the theme *self-control* has for you. Again you will record your summarized impressions in the notebook you are using for this work.

As with all weeks, you want to realize depth and altitude levels of appreciation you have never heretofore glimpsed. You need to make these insights expressive in your meditations and behavior. Your third week opens upon the keynote of *thanksgiving*.

Next, concentrate upon *kindness*, both from the standpoint of God's intention concerning this quality and upon your reflection of its light.

Then should come *reverence*, which merits pondering and active use. During your week on *reverence*, repeat on one day all of the creative methods you have used toward the ripened unfoldment or active participation in the other days.

During your sixth week, let your meditations be upon an *emblazoned love*, all inclusive in range, incisive in energies, being devoted to the good of others for their uplift and encouragement.

Naturally, these last two weeks of this very important six-week cycle, you will particularly pay attention to and include the inner government of mankind; likewise, the great Kingdom of Angels and all the branches of that expression of Divinity. Think meditatively upon humanity as unfolding and receiving the sacraments of this Holy Festival with strengthened enjoyment. During these last two weeks think also of Nature opening its soul, its centers of reception, to the great drafts of spiritual power which will circulate from the inner kingdoms at that time.

The Holy Festival of Christmas should be carefully prepared for. The charging of this remarkable holy-tide is then more readily distinguished. If decorations and household preparations are to be included in your outer festivities, try to have them and all of your other work completed as far as possible by Thanksgiving Day so that your Christmas season can truly open with Thanksgiving. Usually there is too much feverish effort prior to Christmas. This prevents the fullest use of your inner faculties. It is better to attend to your duties with wisdom and with peaceful awareness.

Any sacred season is worthy of your innermost preparation. You are more and more impressed with a desire for a truly spiritual Christmas. See that you spiritualize your own celebration this year beyond all other attempts you have made along these lines. Should you wish ideally to remember others with presents, your giving should be on a day other than our Lord's nativity. You need to discover the true meaning of Christmas and you cannot do this unless the day highlights Christ and is fully consecrated to Him. Family reunions and the joys of gift-giving should come on a day other than the Holy Festival.

181

Christmas rightfully should be celebrated on two days. Let the twenty-fourth of December be devoted to reception and reverence expressed especially for the holy midnight broadcast. The twenty-fifth of December belongs to the practice of consecration to the reality of the Lord Christ. Let every act, word and ideal be consecrated to the universal Presence of the Christ Spirit.

Each Christmas may be a time for the fruits of your aspirations to come to maturity, a garnering of inner harvests. From the noon period of Christmas Day until retirement, endeavor to do all that you can to express the Christ Spirit. By means of goodwill send it into the lives of those who do not as yet have the rich awareness of those transcendent realities.

Do not ever forget that each of you is appointed to a task and is given encouragement for the challenge that is yours through the Brotherhood's interest. Your loves, your labors and enjoyments can only be beautiful if this remembrance is sustained and precedes all other obligations.

An activity of preparation for the holy Christ Festival also stirs the higher worlds. Remember that the nature of your atmosphere is supercharged primarily by the Angel Kingdom. The Shining Ones supply fervency and ecstasy. That which at its lowest point is feeling and at its highest is sublimity of exaltation, flows through these Angelic

182

Beings who are pure beyond man's realization of purity.

Sometimes you receive visitations from Superior Beings who come great distances to witness earth's commemoration of Christ's birth. There are not many planets housing life similar to your own. When this word *many* is used, it is done so relatively, because in nearly every system there are at least two or three planets possessing physical existence. There are relatively few, then, in each solar system with whom the Universal Inner Government can relate.

So at every Christmas season your earth shall receive noble and venerable Visitors. Aspire to see that you and all of humanity are ready for accelerated spiritual energies—ready to receive cosmic tides which bring your planet high Observers with lofty gifts.

As YOU PREPARE for the Lord's Birthday, discover what inward joy accompanies a gift to the Christ Hierarch.

One of you may choose the gift of a pledge to the Christ of continuous, moment by moment striving from December twenty-fourth of one year to the following Christmas Eve of the next year. Another might prefer to pledge himself to an unfoldment of deeper devotion; a third to the conquest of some recognized instability. A fourth might give himself to the transformation of rebirth. Still another might endeavor to give help to others. In all these devotions one's whole nature must be completely and unselfishly absorbed in the fulfillment of the Christ gift until the next Christmas. For that reason the gift needs to be newly and creatively regarded and exercised every day.

Your highest tribute to the Lord Christ is a worship of His Spirit through the *living* of His Spirit. Think His thoughts, be reverent before the fountain of His reality, for then you will realize His love and His pleasure throughout your whole being.

STEPS TOWARD ENLIGHTENMENT

*May the Divine Spirit resident within bring
you to regenerate life.*

IN briefest terms, the inaugural steps toward enlightenment are those which refine, purify, discipline and invigorate the physical and inward
bodies and sensibilities. For this reason much work
is urged upon you for your acceptance of that
which comprises character unfoldment. For this
reason you are led to a revision of your food habits
and the types of entertainment you enjoy. Even
your speech, your gestures, the placement of your
voice, the manner in which you walk, and the conditioning of your thoughts have much to do with
the hastening and the completing of your inner
preparedness for earth's most transforming event.

To us the most needful requisite by which we
judge the probationer's fitness or the disciple's
readiness for further advancement is his aligned
readiness on every plane for the great illimitable
visitation.

We observe many on earth who are ready mentally and spiritually for illumination but they remain unready in their physical forms and in their
astral bodies as well. Until such candidates learn to

wield refining, purifying, spiritualizing will-forces into these lower vehicles, they could not stand the impact of those velocities which are focused upon them at the momentous hour of initiation.

For everyone who approaches conscious or direct knowing there is the intuitional recognition that a certain amount of increasing self-sacrifice, voluntary purification and complete self-surrender is essential. This impression grows upon you and upon any probationer as he nears, in alignment, that preparedness by which his bodies can know the torch of the intensification of Light. We find it difficult to discover on earth, even among the most well-intentioned probationers and disciples, the willingness to practice self-sacrifice of their pet habits and the surrender of their recognized detriments.

Sometimes all that is required for the attaining of the open door into the Kingdom of Light is for a man or a woman to be able in deepest dedication to say "No!" to the appetite, or to say "Be gone from me forever!" to the animal magnetism of personal attraction that appeals to the sensual nature of human beings.

To a few who have an eager and a trained control of their lower natures, the willfulness of pride and of self-centeredness on the emotional and mental planes locks the door to their innermost discoveries.

186

There are no secrets to the awakened devotee. These things each one must have known himself— that illumination comes when the atoms of each vehicle of consciousness have been clarified to a certain point of intensification, appropriate to the initiation. For that reason we urge all students of the Light to entertain feelings, aspirations and adorations of God Light. You must be in love with God Light more than you are with yourself, your appetites, or your material interests, or the bondage that earth holds over you before you become a citizen of the Kingdom of Light through illumination.

Remember foremostly, all that keeps you back from the Light is the curtain of your own indecisions. You are unwilling to part with the wayward things, the temporal, the glamour of outward attractions. You are more fascinated by them than you are by your adventure into Light. Those who find *the quest* and achieve its conquest are probationers who become disciples because expectation runs high in them. The ardor of readiness has already purified them of all these earth-binding elements and they stand, to a given degree, purified of earth's hold.

Any event can precipitate enlightenment—a crisis, a voluntary sacrifice of the lower in favor of the higher, an unselfish deed, a beautiful morning in an elevated state of consciousness. The act, the motivation, or the circumstance which sets off the forces of enlightenment are less important from our standpoint than the conditioning of deliberate expectation and inner preparedness on the part of the novitiate.

Do not be troubled about the ardor required for the intensification of your interest, your worship, and your surrender. Neither should you consider as burdensome your labor for Light. Does not the child come into the world after the mother's nine months of patience and work of delivery? Did not your rarest flower develop and blossom again and again upon a vine which had been nurtured by the slow watchfulness of the loving gardener? The joy of one flowering is more important to him than years of tending the vine. So must you consider the breaking through from one barrier into another dimension. Think only of emergence and let your Soul be filled with gratitude for whatever in qualities of self-conquest or purification can take you to these boundaries of new worlds and new altitudes of consciousness.

Again from our threshold we watch the auras of the probationers and disciples until we observe that every vehicle has, to the limit of the individual's understanding, been as readied and as cleansed as he can make it. And then we wait for the circumstance to bring him upliftment. Occasionally we will precipitate crises which will lift him into a very receptive mood. At the proper moment, when all his vehicles are aligned and all expectant, we send into his aura a strong thermal beam of enlightenment. Everyone greets and welcomes that Light with supernal joy. In our world there are always two attendant Masters in addition to the Guardian Angel at the first initiation. The stream of enlightenment issues, through conscious direction and love, from the Lord of all religions of this planet, Lord Emmanuel, the Christ.

At the second initiation there may be three Masters present, the third officiant being a full representative of the Christ. It could even be the Lord Emmanuel if certain conditions within the pupil made it right that He attend the ordination of this experience.

At the third initiation the disciple-pupil receives not only the impact of the thermal beam of enlightenment directly from the mind and love of the Lord Emmanuel, he likewise knows at-one-ment for the first time consciously with the Lord of the World who is not of earth, whose name among us, as you know, is the Prince of Many Summers, or the Sanat Kumara, the Venusian. His is the love baptism which mingles with the strong accelerations of the thermal beam.

At the fourth initiation, the pupil receives confirmations of blessings from all the Council of Masters because he is soon to take his place among

189

them, and they know how arduous will be his path between the fourth and fifth stages of enlightenment.

At the fifth initiation, which is Masterhood, there is a conscious experience in sight, hearing and attendance in person in Shamballa to which the spirit of the advanced initiate has been taken. He not only sees all his Brothers attending him in his great ritual of accomplishment, but he likewise knows through sight, through at-one-ment, the conscious receiving of new commissions from the Planetary Logos, and behind Him, the strong beam of the Solar Logos. Now he stands a Sun-Initiate, and is under orders not only from his older and more advanced Sisters and Brothers, but from his Supreme Instructor from Whom he must be worthy to take orders at any time—the venerable, majestic, almighty Lord and Logos Osiris, the Sun Logos.

These words are for you to consider and reconsider. The difference between your acceptance and rejection of the Light is sometimes no more than your backward glance into the shadows from which you should have long ago emerged. Know that by your facing the Light you will meet that which the shadows and all your vague dreamings can never even suggest to you—that joy which is from the Source and expresses the supreme and everlasting happiness and power of the Infinitely Highest!

Work well. Be faithful. Give attention to the recollection that you are being watched more continuously than you have realized and that you are being companioned more lovingly than you have ever dared to hope.

May that Light which never fades and the song of inner gladness which sings forever, live immortally in your heart and being.

INDEX